JACK MCLEAN

FOUND

A Veteran Story

Huntington Bay Press

Printed in the United States.

Cover and book design by Asya Blue Design.

ISBN 979-8-9885392-0-9 Paperback
ISBN 979-8-9885392-2-3 Ebook

Published by Huntington Bay Press.

For Nina

...do not take lightly the perils of war.

—Thucydides

PROLOGUE

I am trying to find anybody that might have served with my father Thomas J. Morrissey Jr. He was with C Company, 1st Battalion, 4th Marines, 3rd Marine Division. He was killed on June 5, 1968. Please call me at the number below anytime. Thank you.

—Thomas J. Morrissey III

My mind snapped back forty-one years when I saw the posting on the battalion website. Thomas J. Morrissey Jr. had been my friend. I recalled his thick tangle of black hair, the Ray-Ban aviator sunglasses, and the Zippo lighter that flicked open and shut with each new cigarette that touched his lips. He was the epitome of cool—the guy we all wanted to be.

Tom used to tell us what it was like to grow up in Dover, New Hampshire, with his parents and seven siblings. I was from the

1

Boston area, so we shared a New England tie. He'd also rhapsodize about his wife, Norma, and their young son, Thomas III. On occasion, he'd produce a grainy photo of the two.

"That's some kid, huh," he would say.

"Yeah, Tom," we'd dutifully reply. "That's some kid."

Then he'd point to his wife and say, "Isn't she a knockout?"

And we'd say, "Yes, Tom, she is a knockout," because, in fact, she was.

I recalled the devastating artillery barrage on Landing Zone Loon on June 5, 1968. Shortly after it began, the call went out for volunteers to ferry the wounded to a makeshift landing zone for evacuation. Tom and several others immediately sprang from their fighting holes. I paused. Air bombardments were often followed by ground assaults. I thought some of us should stay in place to defend the perimeter. The last time I saw Tom, several minutes later, he was in a slow-motion jog with a wounded marine slung over his right shoulder. Then, in a flash, he was gone. Thirty-nine other boys were killed during the battle, and another one hundred of us were injured. While those of us who survived were well beyond fortunate, the three days of horror would remain inextricably etched into each of us for the rest of our lives.

A week after I got home from Vietnam in late August 1968, I set out for Dover to see if I could find Norma and their son. Tom's death had left a hole within me. My recollection of his shrapnel-riddled corpse splayed on the barren battlefield triggered my nightmares. As I drove north from Boston, I searched for consoling words I might deliver to her when I got there, but the few that came to mind felt empty. I was alive. Tom was dead. I had been tormented by guilt since that day. Why had I stayed in my hole that afternoon? Why hadn't I carried the wounded up the hill? My mind swirled without resolve for several more miles. *What was I doing?* I now asked myself. *Who was I to think that I could console anyone?* Approaching Dover, I slowed down, made a U-turn, and headed back to Boston.

Over the ensuing years, I'd driven by the same Dover exit on the New Hampshire Turnpike countless times on my way back and forth to Maine. I always thought of Tom, Norma, and their son, Thomas III. On occasion, I'd tapped the brakes in anticipation of taking the exit but never found the courage to do so.

Returning to the present, I stared back at the website posting by Tom's son on the computer screen. I was no longer the guilt-ridden twenty-one-year-old boy who had made that abortive trip to Dover forty-one years earlier. The mental and physical problems that I'd brought home with me had received competent care from the Department of Veterans Affairs, I'd written *Loon: A Marine Story*, a memoir about my Marine Corps service and the battle in which Tom had been killed, which was to be published in two months, and I'd recently reconnected with many of my long-lost brothers in arms. Each of these three elements played a vital role in my recovery. I was stronger now.

Together with my buddies, we brought the dark trauma of our shared past into the light. We began having reunions and, as more of us emerged, recognized that we had not been alone for all those years. We had always had each other. We renewed our faded fidelity to the Marine Corps and reignited our profound pride for having served the United States in harm's way. We vowed to never let anyone take either from us again.

Recovered and recovering, we dedicated ourselves to finding others from Charlie Company who might still be suffering. We knew they were out there. Some were waiting to be found. Others never would be. A select few, however, began reaching out in novel ways, thanks to the growing presence of the internet.

Thomas J. Morrissey III.

I said his name out loud, and the memory of his father washed over me. I thought of Norma—his mother and Tom's widow. The war was not over for either of them. Beneath the website posting, there was a number with a Massachusetts area code. I took a breath, picked up the phone, and thus began a five-year journey that would change the lives of three Vietnam War survivors forever.

Thomas J. Morrissey Jr.

CHAPTER 1

July 28, 1968, Camp Carrol,
Republic of South Vietnam

"I knew a guy in Basic School who went to Harvard," Negron shouted. "He was an asshole."

I could see the trace of a smile through the swirl of red dirt as the helicopter softly touched down, tail first, before me. Our Skipper, Bill Negron, was among a small group of marines gathered nearby. Some, veterans of battles fought together, were there to see me off. Others were recent replacement troops charged with the task of offloading the chopper's cargo.

The instant the front wheels touched the ground, the side-door gunner rested his .50-caliber machine gun, spun around, snatched several large, bright-red nylon mail bags, and threw them out of the hatch. Ten cases of C-Rations, four boxes of M-16 rifle ammo, three crates of 60-mm mortar rounds, and a dozen metal canisters of belted M-60 machine-gun ammo followed. The waiting troops scurried to remove and dispense the cargo, which was the lifeblood of our daily grind. The gunner then signaled to me with a thumbs-up as he regripped his machine gun, chambered a round, and flicked off the safety. I scampered under the still-whirling rotors, scrambled on board, didn't wave, and didn't look back. The whole process had taken less than thirty seconds. Then, in an instant, we were airborne and banking heavily to port as we rose, accelerated, and roared east for the ten-minute flight to the relative safety of Dong Ha, Charlie Company's rear base of operations.

It was July 28, 1968. After nearly ten months in-country, I was going home. In another month, I would be discharged from active duty and enrolled as Harvard University's first incoming Vietnam veteran.

Captain William P. Negron was in his third month as commander of Charlie Company. This was the second of what would become his three tours of duty in Vietnam. The marine from Harvard who he had professed to know in Basic School probably *was* an asshole. No doubt the sentiment was reciprocated since, as I was to discover, these two venerable institutions had little in common. For the rest of my life, the mention of one in the presence of someone from the other prompted open surprise that I had been so closely affiliated with both.

It wasn't always so. Harvard and the Marine Corps had served the United States of America with distinction since colonial times. On the battlefield, only West Point and Annapolis had produced more recipients of the Congressional Medal of Honor. In 1916, Harvard became one of the first universities in the country to offer Reserve Officer Training Corps (ROTC). As recently as 1952, 40 percent of its students were enrolled in programs that would lead to a military commission upon graduation.

Two days earlier, Captain Negron had given me "the talk." In his capacity as company commander, it was his duty to interview each departing marine for the purpose of getting him to reenlist.

"Well, Corporal," Negron began, "here's the offer." The two of us were perched on sandbags at the entrance to his command bunker. "If you agree to extend your enlistment for six months and stay here in-country, *your* Marine Corps will make you a sergeant ..."

That got my attention. *What could be more validating of my service*, I thought, *than becoming a sergeant in the United States Marine Corps?* "No, I don't think so, Skipper, but it's a nice offer." I replied.

"... and assign you to guard duty in Da Nang ..." he continued.

Guard duty in Da Nang was the kind of assignment about which we field grunts could only fantasize. At the time, it was the most secure Marine Corps base in all South Vietnam. There would be cold beer every night, hot chow every day, flush toilets, and perhaps a bed with clean sheets. "Thanks, Skipper. If I weren't headed off to college ..."

"... and," he concluded, "they'll give you another five-day R&R at the destination of your choosing."

That gave me pause. A return to Singapore? The memory of those five fanciful days the previous April still floated through my mind like an apparition. "When could I leave?" I had to ask.

"You can still go the day after tomorrow," he replied. "Either way, you're all done in the field. No matter what you decide, you'll never have to come back to this shit."

The Marine Corps, I thought to myself, *sure knew how to sweet talk a guy.*

Negron half-smiled as our game of cat and mouse played out. He was older than most captains since, like me, he had enlisted after high school. A solid student and a gifted athlete, he had graduated from high school in Perth Amboy, New Jersey, with the class of 1954 and enrolled at Miami University in Ohio. He'd dropped out several months later and returned to New York to pursue a professional boxing career. One morning, after a particularly punishing bout in Madison Square Garden, he walked into a military recruiting office, raised his right hand, and enlisted in the United States Marine Corps.

He returned to Miami University three years later to complete his studies. Upon graduation, he was commissioned as a second lieutenant and sent to Basic School in Quantico, Virginia. The year was 1964. While the Marine Corps would not have an official presence in Vietnam for another year, Negron wanted to be a part of the escalating conflict, so he volunteered for a thirteen-month assignment to serve as an adviser to the South Vietnamese marines. Two years later, in April 1968, he returned to Vietnam to begin his second tour of duty as the commanding officer of my unit—Charlie Company, First Battalion, Fourth Marine Regiment, Third Marine Division.

We both knew that we were lucky to be having this conversation. Two months earlier, nearly half of Charlie Company had been killed or wounded during an intense three-day battle on a remote hilltop near the Laotian border called LZ Loon. The casualties had included Tom Morrissey. Captain Negron had received the Silver Star for valor during the conflict. I had enormous respect for him. Had I elected to reenlist, I might well have forgone Da Nang and remained in the field under his leadership. He was that good.

I thought I saw a faint glimmer of hope in his eyes as he strung me along. Bill loved the Marine Corps, and he liked me. If he thought this was a good decision, he would continue to encourage me. My mind raced. I'd have to find out if college would let me defer my starting date. Then there were my parents. They would not think that this was a good idea.

"Bill ...?" I wasn't sure what to say. I liked the attention and the validation that the Marine Corps conferred by asking me to stay.

"Look, Jack," he said, interrupting my train of thought, "you're going to be starting college next month. *Harvard*, for Chrissake. Thanks for listening to me. I must go through this with every one of my troopers whose time is up. Here, let's have a beer." With that, he reached into a rucksack behind him

10

and pulled out two warm cans of Carling Black Label Beer. He popped both, threw the metal tops over his shoulder, and handed one to me.

"Here's to Charlie Company. *Semper fidelis*," he concluded.

"*Semper fidelis*, Skipper," I replied.

We then rose, set down our beers, and embraced.

I would not see Bill Negron again for twenty-five years.

Bill Negron in Vietnam

CHAPTER 2

August 8, 1968, Brookline, Massachusetts

I came home to a changed America.

A series of startling events had stunned the country since early spring. On March 31, President Lyndon Baines Johnson announced that he would not run for reelection the following November. The unstated reason was the mounting national opposition to the war in Vietnam. The Reverend Martin Luther King Jr., the seminal leader of the civil rights movement, was assassinated in Memphis, Tennessee, on April 4. In response, over one hundred American cities erupted in devastating race riots. On June 5, Senator Robert F. Kennedy (D-NY,) the younger brother of assassinated president John F. Kennedy, was shot while campaigning for president in Los Angeles. He died the next day. That spring, students at dozens of colleges and universities became increasingly vocal and violent in their opposition to the escalating war in Vietnam.

While in-country, we were aware of President Johnson's announcement, the two assassinations, and the burgeoning opposition to the war—we did have occasional access to radios and newspapers—but we tried hard to insulate ourselves from any news that would distract us from our assigned tasks. We had a job to do. Our lives required all the focus that we could muster.

When I did get home, I was astonished by the changes that had occurred. Beer bottles now came with twist-off caps. New cars could be equipped with brain-bending eight-track stereo systems. "Hey, Jude" by the Beatles was the top *Billboard* hit. Two years before, it had been the gushingly patriotic "Ballad of the Green Berets" by Barry Sadler. London Bridge, of nursery rhyme renown, had been sold to a developer who planned to rebuild it—stone by stone—in the Arizona desert.

Two years earlier, in the spring of 1966, I had been a senior at Phillips Academy in Andover, Massachusetts. Little had changed there in decades. An all-boys prep school that had been founded two years after the signing of the Declaration of Independence, Andover graduates routinely matriculated to the country's most prestigious colleges and universities. Both Bush presidents, among other notables, had gone there. In my graduating class, fifty boys went on to Harvard. The numbers for Yale, Princeton, and Stanford were comparable. Decades of prior classes boasted similar numbers. It was expected. It was the reason why parents sent their young sons off to such elite institutions.

After arriving at Andover in the fall of 1961, I joined the school band as a trumpet player. On football Saturdays, as the band had done for decades, we marched down Main Street and up to Brothers' Field. A highlight of our small parade came when we passed the Headmaster's House. Bandleader Bill Clift would give the order to turn "eyes right," and lead us in playing "Brave Old Army Team." Headmaster John M. Kemper, a West Point graduate, would stand at attention on the front steps. I enjoyed playing the trumpet in the marching band. I liked the uniforms (blue blazers and white slacks) and the paramilitary discipline of learning to march in step with several dozen other boys. I also liked playing marches, particularly college fight songs, and always shivered with pride as we entered the football field before a game while playing our school fight song, "The Royal Blue." Having struggled in class during the week, those fall football Saturdays gave me needed structure and made me feel as though I was part of something bigger. I liked the feeling.

On May 30, we marched down Main Street to join the entire school community at the Memorial Bell Tower to honor our nation's war dead. Those Memorial Day parades included several dozen faculty members who were military veterans. Those who could wore their old uniforms. Some were highly decorated, which added solemnity to the occasion. Along our route, we'd play the anthems of each of the four service branches. My favorite was "The Marines' Hymn." At the close of the ceremony in my sophomore year, I was selected to play Taps. It was an unimaginable honor.

The Memorial Day ceremonies filled me with patriotic pride. They also helped me to understand the concept of national service. The faculty members, like most of our fathers, had served our country in the military. We felt that we were part of a continuum and would, like them, soon be called upon to serve as well. The school motto, *Non Sibi* (Latin for *not for oneself*) instilled us with a sense of purpose to serve the greater good.

In the spring of 1966, during my senior year, Andover—like the rest of the country—was on the cusp of enormous social change. The band no longer marched down Main Street on football Saturdays. The Memorial Day ceremony attracted only a smattering of students and faculty. The increasingly unpopular war in Vietnam was taking the air out of publicly recognizing those who had given their lives to create and defend our liberty.

As graduation neared, unlike my classmates, I wasn't eager to attend college right away. I felt that doing something else first for a year or two might be more beneficial. My options were limited, however, since registration for military conscription was compulsory for all eighteen-year-old boys. If you were healthy and not enrolled in high school or college, the chances were good that you'd be drafted. It was the law. My father had served. Respected members of the Andover faculty had served. The extraordinary achievements of recent military heroes like Eisenhower, Bradley, and Marshall still resonated. There was honor in military service. My parents had instilled this in me. Andover had reinforced it. Still, I didn't want to join the military, and I certainly didn't want to fight in a war. But I also didn't want to go to college for the sole purpose of avoiding the draft.

While home on spring break, I decided to depart from the long-established Andover norm and get my military obligation out of the way before starting college. The Marine Corps had a program that required only two years of active duty—the shortest of all the service branches. It seemed right for me, so I raised my right hand and enlisted. I became the first Andover senior in memory to do so. I knew that the Vietnam War was heating up, but few people thought that it would last more than a year or two. I was more concerned about surviving the looming reality of the Marine Corps' infamous Parris Island boot camp.

The Vietnam War escalated rapidly. By October, nearly 80 percent of my graduating boot camp platoon went directly to Vietnam. I was sent to supply school but knew that my days in the States were numbered. In the summer of 1967, I received orders and joined Charlie Company that fall. The next twelve months would become the bloodiest of the war.

I did want to attend college when I returned home, so not long after arriving in-country, during breaks from standing watch in the rain and the mud along the Demilitarized Zone (DMZ) that separated North and South Vietnam, I completed several college applications and sent them off on an outbound supply helicopter.

Now ten months later, having spent the previous week being out-processed at the Treasure Island Naval Station in San Francisco Bay, I was back home in Boston, walking across the tarmac of Logan Airport in the direction of the TWA terminal. I had lost thirty pounds during my year away. My freshly earned combat medals and ribbons hung heavily on the left side of my now-baggy khaki uniform shirt. As I approached the terminal doors, I thought only of my Charlie Company buddies—living and dead. I was coming home to an America that many of them would never see.

It was early evening back in Vietnam. The boys would be digging fresh fighting holes, laying claymore mines, opening cans of C Rations, and setting up the evening watch schedule. I wondered how my former squad mates were getting along without me. Had anyone been killed or wounded since my departure from the field a week earlier? I felt guilty that I was not there.

I thought about Bill Negron and smiled to myself about our last conversation. I thought of fellow mortar-man Dan Burton from San Diego, who had been my "foxhole buddy." He wasn't due to come home until December. I'd worry about him every day until then. I thought of our second platoon naval hospital corpsman, "Doc" Mac Mecham from Novato, California and second platoon machine gunner Wayne Wood from Cedar Rapids, Iowa. I had visited with them in the amputee ward of the Oakland Naval Hospital, where they were recovering from the wounds they received on LZ Loon. I thought of Buck Willingham of Maysville, Oklahoma. Buck had also been a second platoon machine gunner. He was a solid marine with a thick Oklahoma accent and a wry sense of humor that kept us laughing during the darker hours. I thought of Terry Tillery from Canfield, Ohio. Terry and I had joined the second platoon on the same day. Six months later, he became the company radio operator and had been our key communicator during the Loon battle. I thought of Sid MacLeod. Sid had been my best friend through boot camp and my time in the States. We were separated when we arrived in Vietnam in the fall of 1967. He was killed near Khe Sanh the following May. Finally, I thought about Tom Morrissey. I wanted to drive up to Dover as soon as I could to pay my respects to Norma. I wondered what I would say when I got there.

I was fortunate to have survived the year away but didn't feel that way. I didn't feel anything. I was numb. While several people had welcomed me home, no one had thanked me for my service. Americans, in the fall of 1968, did not regard service in the increasingly unpopular Vietnam War as being worthy of thanks.

I felt like Rip Van Winkle, the fictional Washington Irving character who, in the late eighteenth century, fell asleep in the Catskill Mountains and awoke twenty years later to discover that he had missed the entire American Revolution. While I had only been gone for a year, it seemed that another American Revolution had occurred in my absence.

I wanted to stop, right there on the airport tarmac, and give myself more time to take it all in. I knew that once the terminal door opened, a new life would begin, and there would be no turning back.

Corporal Jack McLean USMC

CHAPTER 3

February 1965, Dover, New Hampshire

"Who's that?"

Norma Morrill was sitting in the back seat of her friend Barry Bittner's car. His girlfriend Peggy was in the front passenger seat. Barry was driving slowly down one of the two southbound lanes of Main Street in Dover, New Hampshire, on a snowy slate-gray February afternoon. Norma's attention had been drawn to the handsome young driver of a white Pontiac station wagon that had pulled up on their right side. Despite the bad weather, his window was rolled down, and his left arm was draped out from it.

Barry leaned forward and, looking over to his right, replied, "Oh, that's Tom. Tom Morrissey."

"Whoa, he's cute!" Norma continued. "Do you know him?"

"Yeah," Barry replied. "He's a friend."

Norma's eyes remained riveted on the figure as the two cars

stopped for the traffic light at the corner of Chapel Street. He appeared to be tall and had a thick mop of jet-black hair. His eyes were shrouded by a pair of Ray-Ban aviator sunglasses. The three had planned to drive over to Pease Air Force Base to pick up several airmen for a party they planned to have later that evening at Peggy's house, but off-base liberty had been canceled due to the weather, so they were headed back into Dover to hatch another plan.

"Let's get him to come to our party," Peggy said, her eyes now also fixed on Tom Morrissey.

"Honk your horn!" Norma added with urgency in her voice. Barry obeyed her command and tapped his horn to draw Tom's attention.

Tom looked over. Barry waved. Tom nodded back in recognition.

Peggy rolled down her window. "You want to come to a party?" she said, looking across at Tom.

Pausing briefly, he looked back, absorbed the scene, and responded, "I just got off work. I still have my work clothes on." Tom had just finished an exhausting day of installing siding on a house in the neighboring town of Durham with his father and was looking forward to getting home, taking a shower, and changing into some clean clothes.

"Oh, just come like you are," Peggy said. "It's a blizzard anyway. C'mon. Follow us. We're going over to my house."

"Well, okay," Tom replied with a shrug. Then, as the light changed, the two cars turned left onto Chapel Street and headed for Peggy's place several blocks over on Park.

That was the day that Norma Morrill and Tom Morrissey met.

It was cold. It was snowing. The year was 1965.

Thomas J. Morrissey Jr. was born on August 22, 1948, the second of what would become eight children in the family of Lorraine Flayhan and Thomas J. Morrissey Sr. Tom Jr. and his older brother George were products of Lorraine's earlier marriage to Clifton Locke. When she and Morrissey married in 1949, he not only adopted both boys but also changed Tom's name from Thomas F. Locke to Thomas J. Morrissey Jr.

Morrissey Sr. had been in the navy and now had a small home-contracting business. The family lived in a comfortable house at 24 Lexington Street near the top of the hill in one of Dover's nicer neighborhoods. While he was Irish Catholic, his wife Lorraine, also Catholic, was proudly Lebanese.

When Tom was a year old, his brother Charlie was born and soon diagnosed with cerebral palsy. Although largely able to live a normal life, his special needs added to Lorraine's maternal burden. Five more children followed over the next thirteen years. It became a full and busy house over which Lorraine ruled with an iron hand. She was not a woman to be crossed.

Norma Morrill was born in Middletown, Rhode Island, on June 25, 1948. She had dark-brown hair, hazel eyes, and a bubbly personality. She enjoyed reading poetry, listening to love songs on the radio, and flirting with boys. Norma was quick to see the good in people. Her father had also been in the navy. When Norma was nine, he retired and moved the family—which now included her sisters Debra and Karen—back home to Bangor, Maine, where he bought and ran a convenience store in the neighboring town of Hampden.

A year later, the Morrills divorced. Norma's mother took her two younger daughters and moved three hours south to Dover, which was home to her favorite cousin. Norma remained behind with her father. She attended Hampden Academy and worked in her father's store after school. Most weekends and on school vacations, she would travel the three hours down the Maine Turnpike by Greyhound bus to visit her mother and sisters. It was on one such visit that she met Tom on that snowy winter evening.

The two cars drove to Peggy's house on Park Street. Her family lived on the top floor of a four-family house next to the Dover Footwear factory. Norma's mother and two sisters lived several doors down. This part of town was closely clustered with multifamily frame houses. The neighborhood, several blocks from the Cochecho River, was in the shadow of the huge brick mill buildings that had been built near the falls over a century before.

Norma was smitten the moment she saw Tom. When they got to Peggy's, Norma, Tom, Barry, and Peggy hung around her house for several hours, talking and listening to music on the stereo. Later in the evening, they went down to the Sawyer Mills to park.

"That's when he kissed me for the first time," Norma later recalled. "Girls don't forget moments like that."

Several days after her return to Bangor, Tom mustered his courage, grabbed a pocketful of change, found a pay phone, called Norma, and asked her out when next she visited Dover.

CHAPTER 4

September 1968, Brookline and Cambridge, Massachusetts

I stashed my seabag into the trunk of the family car and slid into the passenger seat next to my father. I twisted around to look at my mother in the back seat. Minutes earlier, I had been taken aback when, as I entered the crowded terminal arrival area, the throng of waiting people grew momentarily silent and parted before me. When I reached my parents, the room let out a collective sigh. Several people clapped. Looking around, I realized that they were all focused on us. While waiting for the plane to arrive, my parents must have told some people that their son was coming home from Vietnam. I often look back at that tender moment as my welcome home parade.

As I recall, we made some small talk on the drive home, but there were few words that could add to the wave of relief that the three of us felt. We lived in Brookline, a forty-minute drive under the harbor and through downtown Boston. As we emerged from the Sumner Tunnel, I spotted the century-old Custom House rising from the center of the financial district. The sixteen-story gothic tower, originally authorized by President Andrew Jackson in 1837, had been the site of my enlistment into the Marine Corps thirty months earlier. How easy it had then been to elevate my right hand and recite the simple oath that had set me off on such a perilous course.

We curved around the Boston Garden and entered Storrow Drive. The Charles River, twinkling in the early morning sun, came into view. A four-man rowing scull was gliding beneath the stately Longfellow Bridge. A Red Line MBTA train climbed between the bridge's car lanes on its way from Charles Street to Kendall Square. This was the moment that I had dreamed about night after endless night in Vietnam.

"Well, dear, how does it feel to be home?" The soft resonance of my mother's voice from the back seat sent a calming wave through me. It was at once so foreign and yet so soothingly familiar that I just wanted the sound of it to hang in the air. My mind flashed back to that raw March afternoon thirty months earlier when I gave her the news that I'd enlisted in the Marine Corps. Her words then were not soothing. "You did not!" she'd stammered as if, by fiat, she could make the whole looming terror evaporate. Now her long maternal ordeal was at an end. I was home. The relief in her voice was palpable. I would never want to do anything that would hurt her again.

"It's the stuff of dreams, Mom," I replied with a stifled half laugh. The words hung in the air as I tried to find others that would more accurately describe how I felt. I wanted to share with her the horror of seeing a dead marine for the first time, or of shooting another human being while being shot at with live ammo, or how frightened I was during those predawn hours on Loon. I had all this stuff pent up inside of me that was bursting to get out. On top of all of that, I missed my buddies. I missed the adrenaline-inducing exhilaration. I missed Vietnam. I missed the Marine Corps. I wanted to share it all with my mother so she could put a bandage on it and make it better. But I never would because I never could.

To ease my transition, I had decided to live at home for the first semester. The alternative was a bunk bed in a freshman dormitory room in Harvard Yard. It was not a difficult decision. After seven years of living in boarding-school dorms, military barracks, and combat foxholes, I wanted to be alone in a quiet space where no one would bother me.

Being at home was a joy at first—or maybe just a relief. With the country outside in turmoil, it was comforting to reenter the family cocoon, where so little seemed to have changed. It was wonderful to see my younger sister Barbara, who had grown into a young woman during my absence. It was also calming to have my parents there. They wanted to know about school, what courses I would be taking—all present-day and forward-looking stuff. There were few conversations about Vietnam once they had confirmed that my limbs were intact and that I was, to their eyes anyway, *compos mentis*. They were proud of what I had accomplished but were not ones, by nature, to linger on the past.

While it had been a long year away for me, it had been an agonizing one for the three of them. Like the families of all kids serving in Vietnam, they had lived day after interminable day not knowing if I was alive or dead. With me now home, they resumed their daily routines with restored peace of mind. On weekday mornings, Barb and Dad walked down High Street to the trolley that would deliver her to school and him to work. In the evening, Mom served dinner at the dining room table.

My older brother, Don, had returned from two years in the Peace Corps and was working for a bank in New York. My older sister, Ruth, had married shortly before I enlisted. She was now teaching second grade in the San Francisco Public Schools and had a daughter, Gretchen, who'd been born while I was in Vietnam. My time away may have been hardest on Barbara. To be attending high school in a region that had become a bubbling cauldron of the burgeoning antiwar movement, while having her big brother fighting the war to which nearly all her schoolmates were fervently opposed, was far from a badge of honor. During my year overseas, consequently, she barely mentioned it. She was aware of no one else in the entire school who had a family member serving in Vietnam.

In the early evening, I'd join my parents in front of the TV to watch the *CBS Evening News with Walter Cronkite.* There were nightly film clips from Vietnam with throaty correspondents covering the battle of the day.

"We'd always look for you," my mother would say.

It would have been a futile effort on her part. The two hundred boys of Charlie Company composed an infinitesimal fraction of 550,000 Americans who were then serving in Vietnam. On Thursdays, the lead story would always be the just-released Vietnam War casualty numbers from the Pentagon. On average, nearly 150 boys were being killed in action each week. There would be news of the campus antiwar protests that were fomenting across the country. Every week or so, there'd be news of yet another American passenger jet being hijacked to Cuba. Then there'd be news of the presidential campaign, which was moving into full swing with Republican candidate Richard M. Nixon of California running against Democratic candidate Hubert H. Humphrey of Minnesota.

One evening, my father asked me who I was going to vote for. This would be my first presidential election.

"I'm not sure," I said. "Whoever makes the war stop and brings all my buddies home."

"That would be Nixon then," my father replied while fiddling with his pipe. "You don't go to the guys who got you into trouble to get you out of trouble."

His reasoning seemed simple enough. Lyndon Johnson and the Democrats had made a mess of things over there. Three months later, I cast my first-ever presidential ballot for Richard M. Nixon.

I didn't care about the war, and I didn't care about the student protests or presidential politics. After several weeks, I didn't care about sitting in the living room, watching the evening news with my parents. I was home and cared about little else. I had four years of college ahead with no sense of what lay beyond. My goal for the past year had been to stay alive. Having succeeded, I had little interest in setting new goals. My outlet was to retreat to my room and study. That would work for about two hours until my mind drifted away from the books and back to Vietnam and my buddies—dead and alive. I missed them. I was still trying to process how, in just two days—eight weeks earlier—forty of them could have been killed—just like that. Where in my addled brain was I supposed to put that horror? I had no good answer, and I knew of no friend or family member who could help me to understand how it was that I had come home alive and they hadn't.

Bedtime brought no relief. I'd lie awake and listen to a local talk radio show, often for hours, to avoid the nightmares that I knew sleep would bring. I also had multiple slivers of shrapnel that had embedded themselves into my right shoulder during the rocket barrage on June 5. The freshly exposed tip of one might catch on the bed sheet when I rolled over, causing a quick, stabbing reminder of the horrific explosion that had interred it there. It would take another ten years for all the shards to either work their way to the surface of my skin or silently settle in for the duration of my life. The recollections of the horror, the loss, and the boys with whom I had shared the experience continually found their way to the surface as well. Unlike the shrapnel, they could not be excised with a pair of tweezers.

In the morning, I'd eat breakfast, drive to Cambridge in a used VW Beetle that I'd purchased, park in the student lot, and walk across the Weeks Bridge to Harvard Yard. By midafternoon, when classes were done for the day, I'd reverse the process and head back to Brookline. Having been out of school for two years, I stayed focused on my studies.

The Harvard University campus bore no physical reminders of my two years away. It thereby became easy at times to imagine that none of it had happened. I could try to forget that I had spent the previous year sleeping on dirt, standing watch at all hours of the night, breathing as one with two hundred other boys, eating C-Rations, burning shitters, and enduring incoming rocket, artillery, and mortar attacks. I could try to forget the sweltering afternoons spent swatting mosquitos with one hand while slashing a machete through virgin jungle with the other. I could try to accept that I would never again fire an M-16 rifle or be lined up in the sights of an enemy AK-47. It was a lot of change to absorb. I hoped that time and the ongoing urgency of academic work would help flush the haunting memories from my mind.

While in the Marine Corps, I always knew what to do—when to sleep, wake up, go to chow, and execute the orders that came my way. I was part of a mission that involved at least two hundred other boys. We each had our assigned responsibilities. Our lives depended upon them being executed with precision. My every second during the previous year had been spent on high alert. Each sound and smell had to be instantly processed.

Jets screamed overhead. Helicopters swooped in with supplies and labored out with the cargo of dead and wounded. Friendly artillery provided constant concussive fire support. We lobbed mortars at the North Vietnamese Army. They lobbed mortars back at us. It was nerve-wracking. It was intense. It was adrenaline producing, and it continued day and night for a year. We could be hit by the enemy at any time. We often were.

All this abruptly stopped when I got home. The deeply embedded survival instincts that had become so well-honed over the previous year, however, did not. I was still constantly scanning the environment for danger. My body remained on high alert. Sudden loud noises could set off a war-zone reaction that forced me to duck, pause, breathe, and refocus. In an instant—while walking across campus, sitting in class, or eating lunch—I could be thrust back into a firefight, jungle patrol, or ambush.

Hard as I tried to forget, I could not shut it out. My brain had become rewired by the trauma that I had endured during the previous year.

CHAPTER 5

September 1968, Boston

She asked if I'd brought a copy of my DD-214.

Weeks back from Vietnam, I had driven to the Veterans Administration offices in downtown Boston to apply for the G.I. Bill.

"Yes," I responded and handed her my discharge paper.

"Do you have two forms of identification?" she continued.

I said that I did and gave her my passport and Massachusetts driver's license.

"And did you bring the certified proof of your enrollment from the college registrar?" she asked.

"Yes," I replied and handed it across to her. It had taken me several hours that morning to find the office of the registrar and have the document produced, copied, and notarized.

"Here," she said, handing me a clipboard with a form attached and a ball-point pen. "Fill this out with your personal information." I thanked her, took the clipboard, and walked over to one of two plastic chairs near the door to complete the paperwork.

After filling in my name, address, and the date, I paused to look around the small office. There was a window on the left that looked out to downtown Boston. The emblem of each service branch was displayed on the right wall. Straight ahead, my eyes rested on the photographic portrait of Lyndon Baines Johnson, the thirty-sixth president of the United States. President Johnson had, until recently, been my commander-in-chief. Now he was only my president. He wouldn't even be that for much longer. The two of us had had a tough year at opposite ends of the military chain of command. Having decided not to run for reelection the previous March, Johnson's portrait would be replaced four months later with one of either Richard M. Nixon or Hubert H. Humphrey.

I recalled the 1964 campaign which Johnson, the incumbent Democratic candidate, had won in a landslide over conservative Senator Barry M. Goldwater (R-AZ). While only four years had passed since that election, it seemed like ages ago. Johnson had promised limited involvement in Vietnam and a dramatic increase in the anti-poverty programs that he dubbed *The Great Society*. Goldwater had called for the use of tactical nuclear weapons in Vietnam and deep cuts in social welfare programs.

With only twenty-three thousand US troops in Vietnam at the time, most Americans weren't concerned about a conflict in a country that they couldn't find on a map. The Democrats had said that Goldwater's policies were dangerous and that he would lead the United States into a real war. "In your guts, you know he's nuts," was one of their campaign slogans. With the memories of World War II and Korea still fresh in the minds of many and the country enjoying the fruits of its postwar prosperity, few people were in the mood for another war. Now, four years later, there were 550,000 American troops in Vietnam.

I completed the form and handed it back to the clerk behind the desk. After a cursory glance, she smiled, nodded in approval, and said that all appeared to be in order.

The G.I. Bill of Rights was created in 1944 to help returning World War II veterans adjust financially to civilian life. It provided, among other benefits, cash payments for college tuition and living expenses. My benefit would be $130 per month, which would cover only a third of my tuition, room, and board. This aroused my first suspicion that the country would neither recognize nor support Vietnam veterans to the same level that they had recognized and supported our World War II and Korean War counterparts. Not only had the educational stipend not kept pace with inflation over the years, but the benefit itself had been routinely cut by Congress as veterans of the earlier wars completed their education.

"When will I hear something?" I asked.

"You should get your first check in a month or two and monthly thereafter for as long as you are enrolled," she said, returning my driver's license and passport.

I started to thank her but instead stood silently in front of her desk.

"Is there something else?" she asked, looking directly up at me.

"No," I said. I paused. "I mean yes. I'm a veteran, and I'm just back from Vietnam. Is there anything else I should know about the Veterans Administration?"

"Such as …?" she replied.

"I'm not exactly sure," I stammered. "What does the VA do?"

"We take care of veterans," she responded, stating the obvious. She then reached over to the side of her desk, picked up a VA brochure, and handed it to me. "Here," she said, "take one of these. It explains everything. Were you wounded while you were over there … or do you have any war-related physical problems?"

"No. Not badly wounded anyway," I responded. "But I did have some skin problems."

"What kind of skin problems?" she asked. "I don't see any mention of medical issues listed here on your DD-214." She was slowly running her finger down my discharge paper, looking for a checked box that she might have missed. I had never looked at my DD-214. It had been handed to me by a harried clerk when I was being out-processed. Days back from Vietnam, I wanted to go home and get on with my life.

There were, in fact, several errors and omissions. Some were inconsequential. Others, like the absence of any mention of the medical treatment I'd received, would come back to haunt me.

"I had open sores and rashes on my face and arms," I answered. "I was taken out of the field for several days to have them treated."

"Okay," she said. "If they recur or something else related to your service comes up, you have one year to file a claim with the Veterans Administration. After that, you're on your own. It's all explained in the brochure."

"Thank you," I said and turned to leave. *One year*, I thought to myself. At twenty-one years old, that seemed like a lifetime.

For the first several weeks after school began, my adrenaline pumped from every pore. I was wired. It was like being back in combat but with no danger of getting hurt. Everything—the courses, the students, the faculty, the dining hall, the freshly mowed lawns—was new, exciting, and invigorating. Hardly a moment passed when I didn't stop to pinch myself to be sure it was all real. With the horror of the past year behind me, I hoped it would never end. I felt safe.

During the day, I attended classes and lectures, researched and wrote papers, kept ahead of the required reading assignments, and spent hours in the library. In the evening, I'd get home in time for dinner, skip the evening news, and retreat to my room to read and review the day's lecture notes. While the nightmares continued, their looming presence now motivated me to stay busier and work harder as I tried to put Vietnam behind me.

But I couldn't. After the initial rush of adrenaline, Vietnam came oozing back in to fill the void at every opportunity. I remained on high alert. It would not leave me alone, and I could not make it go away. Who was I, anyway? I still felt like a marine, but I wasn't one any longer. I was a college freshman, but I sure didn't feel like one of those either. I felt like an imposter. More often than not, I just felt dead inside. I wasn't anybody.

I did want to go out on dates and develop a social life, but to the few girls that I met that fall, I was radioactive—or at least it felt that way. As a former marine, weeks back from fighting in Vietnam, on the Harvard University campus in the fall of 1968, I might well have been dropped in from the planet Neptune. I was also socially inept. Having spent the previous seven years—all my adolescence—under the steadfast thumbs of two strong, all-male institutions—Andover and the Marine Corps, I'd had little opportunity to develop interpersonal skills with girls. My sexual experience had been limited to encounters with two prostitutes.

In early October, the first glimmer of a social life appeared. I met Phoebe at a dorm party after a football game. She was tall, blonde, thin—bordering on skinny—and engaged me in conversation. She was a student at Wheelock College and had grown up in an affluent Boston suburb. I told her that my sister Ruth had also attended Wheelock. I went on to tell her that I was a freshman, had gone to Andover, and had just returned from Vietnam.

"Oh," she said. "I'm sorry."

"Sorry?" I quizzically responded. Why would she be sorry?

"Yes," she reinforced, "I feel so sorry for you."

I *was* having difficulty adjusting, but pity? Was that the vibe that I was emitting? This would become a common theme in my life going forward. People I met might see me as a normal, well-adjusted guy until the word *Vietnam* crept into the conversation. At that point, talk either stopped or, if it went forward, did so awkwardly.

I didn't want to talk with civilians about Vietnam because, as I was to quickly discover, most didn't care, or if they did, didn't know what to say. Neither did I. Conversations often ended with the abrupt question, "Did you ever kill anybody?" Friends, faculty members, and fellow students didn't want to engage with me about Vietnam on anything but a superficial level.

I did yearn to speak with someone, however, who had shared my experience and could help me understand that I *had* fought in a war and that indeed I *had* killed people.

CHAPTER 6

September 1968, Cambridge

W hen I was being discharged, I picked up a brochure that gave a brief introduction to the role of
Veterans Service Organizations (VSOs). I'd given
little thought to them at the time but now wondered if such
an organization might provide me with much-needed guidance
and support.

VSOs are congressionally chartered nonprofits that help
veterans access the benefits and services provided by the
Department of Veterans Affairs and other government agen-
cies. Among the better known of these organizations are the
American Legion, the Disabled American Veterans, and the
Veterans of Foreign Wars. To civilians they are most recog-
nizable as the groups that may organize and participate in
Veterans Day and Memorial Day events in local cities and
towns. The larger ones may have "posts" where veterans can
meet and socialize.

I decided to start with the Veterans of Foreign Wars. I wasn't sure what they did, but since I now *was* one, I felt that they might at least embrace my service and welcome me into the fold. Checking the phone book, I noted that the Cambridge chapter was about a mile from campus. I walked the ten blocks with a bounce in my step. My anticipation grew as I neared the post. I was about to meet other combat veterans who had been through what I was now going through. The building was easy to spot. There was an American flag out front, a prominent logo on the red-brick facade, and inexplicably, a tall replica of a rocket ship on the right-hand side of the tinted glass entry. I walked up the short path, pulled open the door, and entered a sparsely lit room.

Once inside, my eyes had difficulty adjusting. Through a hanging haze of cigarette and cigar smoke, I saw a scattering of older men. Some were drinking at a bar in the corner, two were shooting a game of pool, and several others were playing cards at a table near the door. They all glanced at me, but nobody made a move in my direction. I was suddenly uncomfortable. I didn't feel like I was one of them at all. I felt like what I was—a college freshman dressed in khaki pants, a blue long-sleeved cotton shirt, and brown loafers. They were the older locals. In Cambridge, these two forces rarely mingled and occasionally opposed.

In the fall of 1968, more often than not, the older locals were pro-war or "hawks," and the younger college kids were anti-war or "doves." Since I was part of only a handful of college students in Cambridge at the time who had served in Vietnam, they probably assumed that I was the latter. The national hawk/dove polarity had arisen during the time that I'd been away. I was still trying to understand why I had to have a side in the first place. Unsure about what to do, I walked over to the bar and approached one of the drinkers.

"Excuse me," I began. "Can you help me? I'm a Vietnam veteran. I'm wondering who to speak with. I want to learn more about the VFW to see if I should join."

He looked me up and down, paused, directed his attention to his fellow bar-mates, and responded, "Jimmy's in charge of membership, right?" They nodded in agreement. Turning back to me he said, "Yeah, it's Jimmy. Jimmy O'Callahan. He's not here right now, but he usually comes in for a beer after work, say about five thirty or six. Why don't you come back then?"

Nobody offered me a beer. Nobody invited me to join the card game. Nobody waved me over to the pool table. Nobody welcomed me home. Not even these fellow veterans.

"Okay, thanks," I said and headed back to the door and the sunshine beyond.

I was not naïve. When I first got home, I knew from others who'd returned before me that my service might not be respected by most Americans. I also knew that there might be people who identified me with the war—perhaps they'd call me a baby killer. I was prepared for that. I was, after all, the only person that most people knew who had been to Vietnam. I was an anomaly. What I was not prepared for was the ambivalence I felt from these veterans of other foreign wars. I felt that they might at least welcome me into the tribe. But they didn't. Once again, I felt alone and isolated.

On my way out, I picked up a pamphlet from a box that was attached to the wall near the door. I then walked down the street to a small park, sat on a bench, and opened the brochure to see what I might learn about the organization's history and purpose. I learned that the VFW had been founded by Spanish-American War veterans, many of whom returned home in 1898 wounded or sick, at a time when there was neither medical care nor pensions for war veterans. Its purpose was to assist and advocate for veterans and war widows while promoting "Americanism."

I understood the "assist and advocate" part, although given the beer-drinking, pool-shooting, and card-playing that I had witnessed, this part of the mission had not been evident inside the post. I did not understand the "promoting Americanism" part. It felt suspiciously hawkish to me. I didn't want to be part of something that was advocating for either side—hawk or dove. I just wanted to talk with someone who might understand what I was going through. I surmised that what I was looking for was not to be found within the walls of the Cambridge chapter of the Veterans of Foreign Wars. I never entered a VSO again. Not even once.

I soon learned that the same feeling was being shared by the tens of thousands of other veterans who were returning to their hometowns across the country each week. Americans, it appeared, were associating those of us who had fought the Vietnam War with the national policy that was executing it. This was new ground, since our country had never fought an unpopular war. Relatively few Vietnam veterans, consequently, were drawn to the VFW or the other existing VSOs. It remained that way for years—until well after the war had ended. Long the private purview of World War II and the Korean War veterans, they were not interested in opening their doors to what many saw as a ragtag group of Baby Boomers. They had won the Big War, after all, while we were to become the first generation in American history to lose a war.

Over time, however, I learned that there was more to it than that—much more. The nationwide indignation directed at Vietnam veterans was being systemically exacerbated by the very institution that had authorized the war in the first place—the Congress of the United States. It took me years to understand that which might have been obvious back in the fall of 1968. Not only had our military service been belittled by the American people, but we had also been estranged from the three institutions that had been charged with supporting us. The Veterans Service Organizations, the Veterans Administration, and the Congress had, for years, worked at purposes that were at odds with the effective treatment of the medical and readjustment issues we faced.

These three groups had long been locked into what had become known as the "Iron Triangle," a triumvirate led by Congressman Olin "Tiger" Teague (D-TX), a decorated World War II veteran. Teague had been entrenched as the chairman of the House Committee on Veterans Affairs since 1955. Under his direction, Congress, the VA, and the VSOs made up a cabal that catered almost exclusively to the needs of World War II and Korean War veterans. The VSOs proposed generous legislation to benefit these veterans in each congressional session. The Congress then usually passed it, and the VA doled it out, often without regard to real need. During that time, with the support of the united VSO bloc, Congressman Teague successfully stalled *every* attempt by Congress to enact *any* piece of legislation that would address the immediate and pressing needs of returning Vietnam veterans.

Most Vietnam War veterans, like me, came home alone and were dropped, unprepared, into a society that neither cheered their return nor admired their service. When I left Camp Carroll the previous July, I had been the only member of my unit to leave the field that day. Two days later, I came home alone to an America that had no more of an idea of what to do with me than I did with it. This included my family and close friends.

When, in the late 1960s, the first group of Vietnam War veterans approached Congress to make the case for some form of readjustment counseling, Chairman Teague called us "a bunch of crybabies."

It would take years for the growing legion of Vietnam veterans to even get a fair hearing before Congress.

Two events served to compound the negative feelings that many Americans held toward Vietnam veterans. The first was the horror of the My Lai Massacre. The other was the campaign strategy employed by the Vietnam Veterans Against the War.

On March 16, 1968, Second Lieutenant William Calley Jr., a platoon leader in C Company, First Battalion, Twentieth Infantry Regiment, Eleventh Brigade of the Twenty-Third Infantry Division, ordered his troops to conduct an assault on the defenseless South Vietnamese hamlet of My Lai. They killed as many as five hundred women, children, infants, and old men who put up no resistance. Only one American soldier was reportedly injured, this due to a malfunctioning weapon. Many of the women and girls were raped and their bodies mutilated. Senior US Army officials succeeded in covering up the incident for over a year.

The atrocity sparked horror and outrage at home and abroad. Serious questions arose in all quarters about America's conduct of the war and, of more consequence to returning veterans, the emotional stability of those of us who were doing the fighting. After My Lai, it became increasingly common to hear of Vietnam War veterans being referred to as "baby killers."

Concern about our emotional stability was unintentionally amplified by a group of returnees who, in 1969, formed the

Vietnam Veterans Against the War. It was the first time in American history that returning veterans had actively and openly opposed a war that was still being fought. To dramatize their cause, the group focused on directing public awareness to what they alleged was the gross misconduct of American combat troops. They thought this strategy would bring the horror of the war home to the American people. These deplorable actions by our troops, they asserted, rose to the level of war crimes and were evidence that poor leadership from the top down was responsible for the atrocities that they professed to have witnessed.

While in Vietnam, I never saw or even heard of any behavior by American troops that rose to the level of an atrocity—not even close. Now, however, people were asking me what I thought about them with the assumption that I must have some firsthand knowledge.

While the efforts of the Vietnam Veterans Against the War may have succeeded on some levels, an unintended consequence was that they contributed to a lasting impression among many that our combat troops were a bunch of out-of-control crazies who routinely torched villages and committed heinous atrocities.

CHAPTER 7

May 1965, Dover

After several months of enduring the long waits between dates, Tom began to devise ways to get himself up to Bangor. Early on, he'd borrow his aunt Mickey's car. As his confidence grew, he'd make up excuses to borrow his parents' station wagon for the six-hour round trip.

"Tom used to get into a lot of trouble coming to Bangor to see me," Norma later recalled.

The more serious their young love became, the more Tom's mother, Lorraine, protested. She was unwilling to cede even an ounce of her son's affections to this teenaged interloper. Still, the more Lorraine pushed, the more Tom pushed back.

"If she'd just left us alone," Norma later recalled, "we probably would have broken up after a few months, like most kids." But they were young, stubborn, and falling in love. They felt that there was no wall tall enough to keep them apart and, as their life evolved over the next two years, this largely held true.

That May, as prom night approached in Dover, Tom announced to his parents that he had a date. They were thrilled. This certainly meant that the absent Norma was drifting out of his life and a new love interest was entering. They offered him the family station wagon for the evening, helped him with the tuxedo rental, and provided a corsage for his date. The only condition was that he bring her by the house beforehand so they could take some pictures of the happy couple.

When the evening came, Tom purposely dawdled in his preparations.

"I'm late, Ma," he said as he hastily came down the stairs in his tuxedo. "I won't have time to bring her by. I'll get someone at the dance to take a picture of us."

With a wave of his hand, Tom scooped up the car keys and corsage and headed for the back door. After carefully laying the corsage on the front passenger seat, he backed out of the driveway, turned on the car radio, and headed to Bangor.

"He gave me the corsage. We just sat on a bench by the river, and we talked until about ten o'clock," Norma later recalled. "We embraced, and he drove the three hours home to Dover." It was a moment that neither would ever forget—both exhilarating and painful. *How much longer could this go on?* she thought. The unbridled joy that she felt each time he arrived was continually trumped by the crippling pain that overwhelmed her each time he left.

A month later, Tom borrowed his aunt Mickey's Mustang and drove back up to Bangor for the afternoon. As he was getting ready to head back home, Norma turned to him and said, "Let's run away."

"Run away?" Tom replied. "Run away where?"

"Just away. Away from this," she said with a broad wave of her hand. "Away from your mother, away from, well, everything."

"Where would we go?" asked the unsure but increasingly interested Tom.

"Boston," Norma responded. "We could go to Boston. Rick lives in Somerville, just outside of the city." Norma's mother had remarried a gentleman named Rick Gardner several years before. While they were now separated, he had been adored by both Norma and Tom and supportive of their burgeoning relationship.

"Come on. Let's go there," Norma concluded. "I have his phone number. It will be fun. Rick will understand."

Norma could be persuasive. Without further pondering, Tom acceded. He gave scant thought to having to show up to work with his father the following morning and no thought to returning Mickey's car. Of course, she would understand. While Norma's father had just left for the evening, she bore little if any concern about having to open the convenience store the next morning. Certainly, her father would also understand. So, with all the sense that God gave teenage lovers, no plan, little money, and half a tank of gas, they hopped in the car, put the top down, turned on the radio, and headed south for the four-hour drive to Somerville. They were free at last.

They had no map and did not know Rick's address, but Tom thought he knew the way, having driven to Boston several times since he'd gotten his driver's license the year before. Three hours after leaving Bangor, they crossed over the Piscataqua River into New Hampshire. Fifteen miles later, having sped by the Dover exit and thrown a quarter into the Hampton toll basket, they approached the turnoff for Rye Beach.

"We could just go to the beach," Tom offered. "I know a place where we could spend the night." Tom loved the beach and spent every free summer hour there.

"No," Norma replied, "let's really get away. The beach is too close to home. Besides, we have no money and not much gas. Rick will help us out. It's not too much further." So, they passed into Massachusetts, cut across Route 128 to Reading, then headed back south on I-93 until it ended at the Somerville-Medford line. They pulled over at the first phone booth they saw outside the Assembly Square Mall. Norma took the slip of paper with Rick's number on it from her wallet, put in a dime, and made the call. No answer. She hung up. The coin returned. She called again. No answer. Either he wasn't home or she had the wrong number. The slip of paper had become heavily creased in her wallet and hard to read.

As evening fell, with no money for gas, food, or a place to stay, Tom pulled the car over to the back of the parking lot that ran along the Mystic River behind the Jordan Marsh department store. There they waited. Every hour or so, Norma would walk back over to the phone booth and try the call, to no avail. Soon they pulled up the convertible top and squeezed into the back seat for the night.

When the next day dawned, they continued the routine. Tom lowered the top and Norma made regular trips over to the phone booth. They had no choice but to either wait until Rick answered the phone or ... well, there was no "or." With the gas tank nearly empty, they couldn't even drive the hour back to Dover.

The ordeal ended late that afternoon when a Medford police cruiser pulled alongside the Mustang and stopped. The officer got out, asked for their identification, radioed in the car information, and soon returned with the verdict. Both had been reported as missing persons and had been the objects of a search which, by this time, spanned several northeastern states. Ordered out of the car, Tom raised the convertible roof, locked the doors, and joined Norma in the back seat of the police cruiser. The two lovers were then driven to the nearby Medford Police Station and placed in adjoining locked rooms where they were told to remain until their parents came to pick them up.

Although exhausted, they spent the first hour standing on their chairs, talking and laughing through a shared vent near the ceiling. Soon the reality of the situation began to sink in, however, as they wondered which parents would show up and when. Two hours later, they had their answer. Norma heard Lorraine's screaming voice as the neighboring door was opened and slammed closed.

She was furious.

Several hours later, Norma's father arrived.

It was a long drive back to Bangor.

CHAPTER 8

January 1968, Cambridge

I thought about my "foxhole buddy" Dan Burton a lot that fall. He'd been scheduled to come home in December. We'd exchanged several letters in the months since my return. His descriptions of the miserable day-to-day existence of our Charlie Company buddies were heart-wrenching. He said that they were continuing to endure steady action in the sweltering heat. He wrote about the fresh losses they were suffering—dead and wounded. Some had been friends. I'd continue to wonder from the comfort of my room how *I'd* ever survived the experience.

To bring the company back up to strength, he said that fresh stateside marines were arriving nearly every day. When a new guy arrived, one of the old timers would take him under his wing for a few days and show him the ropes. He'd be cautious, however, about getting too close. No one wanted to make a new friend who, within a matter of weeks, could be dead. The camaraderie that we'd had prior to LZ Loon had evaporated.

Dan was also disheartened by the increasingly bad news from home. He wondered how he would readjust to civilian life in a country that seemed to be spinning out of control. The bright-eyed optimism and infectious good humor that had kept me going day after endless day were not to be found in Dan's writing that fall.

The last letter I got from Dan came in early December, shortly after he'd returned home to San Diego. He said that he would be serving out the final months of his two-year tour up the road at Marine Corps Base Camp Pendleton. "Nothing is the same. San Diego is unrecognizable," he wrote. He went on to say that the once-proud military town now treated its returning vets "like vermin." When he connected with his old high school friends, he found them to be "immature, particularly with regard to political and worldly issues." Chris Ward, the love of his young life, with whom he had spent five idyllic days on R&R in Hawaii only four months earlier, seemed distant. Their relationship, which had once been fluid and easy, had become awkward and strained. He decided to break up with her. "If you love something, set it free," he said. "It was the war," he remarked, "the fucking war." While he said that he felt like the same Dan inside, he soon realized that, in the eyes of others, he wasn't. Like me, he didn't know who he was anymore.

Dan had given me his mother's telephone number, so I called her in late January to see how I could get in touch with him. She knew who I was from Dan's letters home, so before giving me his number, she wanted to hear all about my new life. She asked about college, my family, and even my love life. She told me that Dan was having a tough time readjusting. She was concerned about his welfare. She hoped that I might be able to cheer him up.

When I called him later, I was excited to hear the sweet sound of his voice for the first time in four months but taken aback by his underlying melancholy.

"You okay, my brother?"

"Not really," he responded. "I mean, it's good to be back and all, but …" After a pause, he suddenly became animated. "Hey, I got to tell you about my bitchin' homecoming."

"Bitchin'?" I repeated. From his last letter, it didn't sound like there was anything about his homecoming that had risen to that level.

"Yeah, well, wait until you hear this," he began. Did I tell you I had malaria?" Barely pausing, he began to tell me the story.

In October 1968, while reading a candlelit book in his bunker, Dan told me that he'd been bitten by a mosquito. He remembered feeling the bite, slapping the offending bug, and seeing the ensuing dribble of blood.

"I was reading that copy of *Valley of the Dolls* by Jacqueline Suzanne that you gave me before you left," he added.

We had all been bitten by mosquitoes countless times during our tours. It was a bother, not unlike the scampering rats that interrupted our sleep. To protect ourselves, we lathered high-intensity bug juice on our exposed skin and swallowed golf ball–sized pink malaria pills once a week. Mosquitoes in Vietnam were like the ones back home, except that they carried an array of potentially deadly diseases. Swatting one could, thereby, be an act of survival, not just a way to avoid an irritating itch.

Several days later, with the itch gone and his memory of the bite fading, Dan awoke from a deep sleep shivering, delirious, and drenched in sweat. Shortly after dawn, he was medevacked to Delta Medical in Quang Tri, our rear base of operations. After a quick checkup, he was loaded onto another chopper and flown to the USS *Repose* (AH-16), a hospital ship that lay at anchor in the South China Sea near Da Nang. There he would remain, bedridden with malaria, for the next three weeks.

In early December, a thinner and weaker Dan was declared fit for duty and ordered to return to Quang Tri for reassignment to Charlie Company. It was not a prospect he relished. With only a month left in his tour, Dan had already been more fortunate than most. The previous May he had been transferred from the second platoon into my 60-mm mortar unit. It turned out to be an extraordinary piece of good luck. Several weeks later, during the battle for LZ Loon, nearly all of his former platoon, including Tom Morrissey, had been killed or wounded.

When Dan returned to Quang Tri from the *Repose*, he reported to the Charlie Company clerk.

"Corporal Burton reporting ... without enthusiasm," he said to the lance corporal sitting behind the duty desk.

"Burton ... let's see," he responded, while fumbling through the stacks of files that littered his desktop. "Okay, here you are. Burton ... sixty mortars, right?"

"Yup," Dan responded.

After opening the file and scanning the contents, he continued, "Looks like you still got a month left. That sound about right?"

"Yup," Dan murmured.

"Geez, you look like shit," the clerk said, looking up. "What happened to you? Malaria?"

"Yeah," Dan replied, "I've been down vacationing on the *Repose*."

"Bummer." the clerk concluded. "I'm glad you came out of it okay. Grab your gear. You can probably get back to the field on the mail chopper this afternoon."

With that, Dan picked up his pack, grabbed his rifle, dropped his head, and shuffled to the door. Once outside, he briefly paused to let it all sink in. *Back into the shit*, he thought.

"Hey, Corporal. Corporal Burton?" The voice floated up from behind him. When he turned, he saw the company clerk standing in the open door of the hooch. His face held an expectant expression. Dan stared at him, lost in his thoughts, but said nothing.

"Corporal, you want to go home?" he asked.

Dan stared back at him, stupefied.

"Look," the clerk went on, "I got this request from on high the other day. I almost forgot about it. They're looking to fill a plane with short-timers for something called 'Christmas Out of the Foxhole' in Phoenix, Arizona. We're allowed to send one guy from the company. The deal is that you go to Phoenix for five days of festivities then you're free to go home on leave. You'll be done with Vietnam. You want to go?"

Dan stood in frozen disbelief before quickly stammering, "Shit, yeah!" He didn't understand what was going on, but he did understand home. "When do I go?"

"Now," the clerk replied. "I mean right now. You've got to get your ass down to Da Nang this afternoon. The plane leaves first thing in the morning."

Dan accompanied the company clerk back into the office, signed some forms, and left clutching a white manila envelope that contained his hastily constructed official orders. He then turned in his rifle and pistol at the armory tent, reclaimed his sea bag from the supply tent, and hustled off to the landing strip.

In earlier wars, returning combatants usually came home with their units on troop ships. During the weeks that it took to get back to the States, they'd have ample time to process with their buddies the things they had together endured. The coming-home experience of Vietnam veterans, however, was in stark contrast. Most came home alone and could be back in the States within a day or two after leaving the field. This difference has since been given as a reason why the incidence of PTSD was so much higher among Vietnam veterans.

The common narrative about returning Vietnam veterans was that there were no parades to welcome us home. That was mostly true, but not entirely. Dan Burton, along with a planeload of others, was unwittingly manipulated into playing a staged role in the divisive politics of the times. *They* had gotten a parade.

"Let's just say that it didn't take me long to realize that things had gotten a little political since I left," Dan told me.

Two days later, a PanAm charter filled with Dan and two hundred other dumbfounded returning Vietnam veterans touched down in Phoenix's Sky Harbor Airport. As the cabin door opened, Dan was seared by the dry desert heat that came rolling down the aisle. It was a welcome relief from the thick, wet jungle heat of Vietnam. He'd never been to Phoenix but was now closer to San Diego and home than he'd been in a year. All he had to do to get there was survive the next three days.

Dan uneasily descended the first two steps of the mobile stairway that had been pushed up to the plane door. His legs were weak, and his eyes were temporarily blinded by the midday glare of the Arizona sun. Once he was able to focus, he saw a receiving line at the bottom of the steps. A group of men, some in uniform, were shaking the hand of each disembarking returnee. Dan recognized Arizona Republican Senator Barry Goldwater whose shock of white hair and thick, black-framed glasses had made him instantly familiar to millions of TV-watching Americans.

Goldwater had hit the national stage four years earlier during his unsuccessful bid for the presidency. Although he had lost to Lyndon Johnson in the largest landslide in American history, he remained the respected conscience of most American conservatives. Vietnam had not been a major issue in the 1964 campaign, but Goldwater's staunch anti-Communist views caused many voters to fear that, given the chance, he might have been militarily adventurous. Now, four years later, forty thousand American boys were dead, the nationwide anti-war movement was raging, and President Johnson had decided not to run for reelection. The newly-elected Richard M. Nixon would be inaugurated in a matter of weeks. Although nobody knew it that day, the war would continue for another seven years. Dan now thought that Goldwater didn't look so scary after all.

Goldwater was joined on the tarmac by several high-ranking military officers and some older civilians in dark suits. Looking toward the terminal, Dan noticed a cluster of several hundred civilians behind a barricade, smiling, waving, and holding up "Welcome Back" signs. He also saw dozens of cheering young women. The organizers had apparently enlisted a contingent of University of Arizona coeds to join in the festivities.

"Welcome back, Corporal." Goldwater stood straight, looked Burton directly in the eye, and had a firm handshake. Before he could respond, Goldwater was focusing on the next guy coming off the steps. Down the line he went. A general, several colonels, and Milton H. Graham, the mayor of Phoenix (as Dan later learned), all proffered their hands, cheerful greetings, and attaboys.

The next few days passed in a blur. The returnees were given money to buy civilian clothes and incidentals, housed in a nice downtown hotel, and shown around town by the coeds. When their buses arrived at the hotel, most of the exhausted boys found their rooms and went right to bed. Others ran directly into the bar. A handful, however, seeing an unexpected opportunity, grabbed the money, hired a taxi to drive them to the bus or train station, and beat it for home.

I asked Dan how all of this made him feel.

"Oh man, Jack," he responded, "you have no idea. It was total bullshit. All these politicians wanted to put on this big public show of support both for the war and the troops. I felt like a pawn in this big game between the hawks and the doves."

"Why did you stick around? I mean, how come you didn't beat it home like those other guys?" I asked.

"Yeah, good question," he said. "Maybe I should have, but I was exhausted. After a year in 'Nam, I figured I could play along for five more days. I mean, it wasn't exactly heavy lifting. They were going to put us up in a nice place, feed us great chow, and march us in a parade through downtown. Oh, and did I tell you about the coeds? Bitchin'!"

Days before, Dan had been recuperating from malaria on the *Repose.* Now, having had little time to process any of it, he found himself thrust into the rancorous national political tug-of-war between Vietnam War hawks and doves.

Over the next several years, Dan and I spoke a half-dozen times. I would usually call after a night of drinking while sitting alone in my room being tortured by vivid flashbacks. Each time I'd have to wake up his mother to get his new number. "Do you have any idea what time it is?" would be her sleepy greeting. I'd have no answer since I usually didn't have a clue. She knew the dark depths of her son's emotional state and, by now, probably assumed mine to be the same. She understood that we needed each other.

During those late-night conversations, Dan and I would talk about our current lives, which could not have been more different. I was in college trying to get myself from book to class to term paper to exam. He'd thought about returning to college but was unable to motivate himself to do anything. We rarely spoke of Vietnam. It was over. We had survived. Nothing in our lives would ever again be so awful. If our conversation did briefly turn to the war, it was only to wonder what had become of the others. I thought that Dan was a lost soul, not realizing at the time that I was as well.

Over time, Dan and I stopped talking altogether. Having been inseparable for nearly a year, we'd quite simply run out of things to say. There was no path forward. The war was all we had.

We would not reconnect for thirty years.

Jack McLean & Dan Burton

CHAPTER 9

February 1969, Cambridge

When the first semester ended in late January, I felt confident and relieved. My grades were good, and the focused daily intensity on my studies had—but for the now-diminishing flashbacks and nightmares—helped keep my memories of Vietnam at bay.

During the weeklong break between semesters, I sold my car, bought a stereo, and moved into a vacated single room in Elliot House, one of a dozen dormitories on campus that were restricted to upperclassmen. My new housemates were closer to my age and helped me feel that I was now part of the college community. I joined them for meals in the dining room, studied with them in the house library, partied with them on weekends, and heeded their valuable advice about which courses to take and which professors to avoid.

Some of my new friends asked me about Vietnam, but most didn't seem to care. I was, after all, a prescient reminder of the fate they faced after graduation when their student draft deferments expired. A few, however, were incredulous that I had not only served in the military but had volunteered to do so. I could have ducked it, they said, by getting a letter from a doctor, or by going to Canada, or by using family connections to get into the National Guard. To many of them, my two-year enlistment in the Marine Corps was seen not as honorable national service, but as a flaw in personal judgment.

I had never doubted my decision to join the Marine Corps and, despite the growing unpopularity of the war on campus and around the country, was proud of my combat service in Vietnam. I did care about what other people thought and did want to be respected for what I had accomplished, but as time went on, had no expectation that that would ever happen outside of a small number of friends and family. It remained that way for decades.

In February 1969, weeks into the second semester, I met Jayne Budura, a sophomore at Boston University. Jayne was striking—tall with an endless smile, luminescent dark eyes, and straight brown hair that cascaded over the top of her shoulders. I was smitten from the moment we met. On our first date, we walked to a nearby Italian restaurant, lingered over a dinner of pizza and beer, and spent the evening in unbroken conversation. I couldn't get enough of her. I wanted to know about her life, her parents, her three sisters, the courses she was taking, and what she thought about any subject that she cared to introduce. I was transfixed by the sweet tenor of her voice.

She wanted to know about me as well but soon dwelled on Vietnam. Why had I enlisted? What had Vietnam been like? Jayne asked question after question that delved into my recent unexamined past. As the evening wore on, she brought some of it to the surface—piece by agonizing piece. She listened and she cared. Jayne was smart, talented, and intellectually curious. I never wanted the evening to end. That Friday, we went out again.

Over the following weeks and months, Jayne filled an emotional abyss and became my guide through the bewildering social changes that were taking place all around us. When I had a flashback or became rattled by some external stimulus, she'd initiate a loving hug and talk me through it. When present for one of my nightmares, she'd gently soothe me like a mother with an infant child. Jayne was the first civilian who not only cared about my Vietnam experience but knew how to access and deal with the hidden parts of my soul where the haunting memories lurked.

With her companionship and guidance, I rejoined our generation. I let my hair grow and my appearance became more relaxed—verging on unkempt. We smoked pot, wore bell-bottom jeans, listened to "Aquarius/Let the Sunshine In," and imagined a world in which only the two of us existed. She got excellent grades, wrote poetry and screenplays, joined a sorority, played "Martha My Dear" on the piano, and picked folk ballads on her Martin guitar. The world was a mind-expanding learning experience for Jayne. I was in love for the first time.

The Harvard University that I entered in the fall of 1968 had changed little in the previous decades. While women from neighboring Radcliffe College had recently been admitted into the classrooms, the administration, faculty, and culture remained largely male and conservative. There were, however, two explosive issues simmering under the surface that fall. By mid-spring, they had turned the university on its ear. The first involved Harvard's increasingly tense relationship with its Cambridge and Boston neighbors. Like many universities, they had been pushing their geographic borders into local neighborhoods for years. The other bubbling issue was the increasing student opposition to Harvard's institutional involvement with ROTC. Most undergraduates were, by the winter of 1969, opposed to the war in Vietnam. ROTC, as physical evidence of Harvard's support of the government and thereby the war, became an obvious target.

On the evening of April 8, 1969, a group of students marched to the home of President Nathan Pusey and tacked a list of demands to his front door. On the following day, absent a response to the demands from the administration, some three hundred protesting students stormed into and occupied University Hall, Harvard's main administration building.

The breadth and intensity of the student protests that spring brought the Vietnam War back into my world. I was angry at the protestors, many of whom I saw as privileged little flag-burning, draft-dodging shits. Others, however, I'd known since Andover. It was confusing. I retained a deep affinity with my brothers in arms who had fought and were still fighting in Vietnam, respected the American flag under which I had proudly served, and was grateful to Harvard for the opportunity that they had given me. The following morning, before dawn, armed and helmeted members of the Massachusetts State Police poured into Harvard Yard, stormed University Hall, and using billy clubs and mace, forcibly removed the demonstrators.

That summer, Jayne joined her family on a six-week cross-country car trip. I moved out of the dormitory and rented a spare room in a run-down house in the neighboring city of Somerville. My roommates were two Harvard medical students with whom I had nothing in common. I remained there for two years.

To support myself, I got a job driving a Checker taxicab in Boston. It was fun for a while. I spent my days navigating around Boston, meeting all manner of people. I enjoyed the freedom. I could drive when and where I wanted and was subject to no higher authority. I didn't make much money, but got to know Boston's buildings, streets, and alleys like the palm of my hand. Absent Jayne, however, my mind was free to wander, and, in idle moments, still drifted back to Vietnam. I might hear a helicopter where there was none, see a nonexistent strafing jet screaming across an empty afternoon sky, or smell fetid summer odors that took me right back to the jungle. Those moments made me realize not only how much I missed Jayne, but also the degree to which I had come to rely on her comforting support.

One hot summer evening, I came home to an empty house, opened a bottle of beer, and flipped on the TV in time to see *Apollo* 11 Mission Commander Neil Armstrong step down the ladder from the lunar module *Eagle* and place his left foot on the surface of the moon. It was 9:12 p.m. on July 20, 1969. "That's one small step for man, one giant leap for mankind," he said. While American boys had spent the previous four years fighting and dying in a pointless war, the country's most gifted minds had figured out how to land two men on the moon, return them safely to Earth, and show it all on live television! It was mind-blowing.

Eighteen American boys were killed in Vietnam that day. The contrast was palpable. During my year back home, I had grown increasingly opposed to the war and was furious at the Nixon administration that could not get us out. American boys—just like I had been—were still dying every day.

Jayne returned from her family trip in early August. We happily picked up where we left off and spent a dreamy autumn commuting on weekends between her sorority house on Commonwealth Avenue in Boston and my house in Somerville. All seemed perfect. There were storm clouds on the horizon, however. Jayne had received a fellowship to attend Oxford University for the coming spring semester. Our perfect life together was about to change dramatically.

In January 1970, she left for England.

CHAPTER 10

Summer 1965, Dover

By the end of their junior year, it had become obvious to Norma that she and Tom could no longer be separated, so she decided to move in with her mother and two younger sisters in Dover. The space would be tight. She would have to support herself and help her mother with money, chores, and the care of her two younger sisters. But she would be near Tom, so it was worth it.

In her absence, Tom had become a daily visitor to her mother's Park Street house. He'd do odd jobs, fix the things that had to be fixed, paint the porch, and just hang out with Debra and Karen. Sometimes he'd come in his aunt Mickey's convertible, wearing his signature Ray-Ban aviator sunglasses. Norma's younger sister Debra, twelve years old at the time, had long blonde hair. He'd say, "Don't ever cut your hair." Then he'd take her out for ice cream. All her friends would watch them ride down the road. Debra adored him.

Norma arrived in Dover early one August morning with only a suitcase and, exhausted from the trip and lack of sleep, went right to bed. Later that morning, when Tom came by for a visit, Norma's mother suggested that he peek in the bedroom. While casting a quizzical look, he carefully opened the door. There she was, sound asleep.

"I came down and got there early in the morning, so I went to bed at my mother's house," Norma later recalled. "Tom came to visit my mother and she said, 'Go look in the bedroom.' He didn't know I was coming. And it was raining, I remember that. He had shorts on. He was stopping there on his way to the beach, but it was raining, so he stopped to see her."

After seeing Norma asleep in the bed, he gently closed the door, walked back out into the living room, and looked to her mother for some affirmation. She smiled and nodded. "Yes, Tom," she said, "she's here for good."

With that, Tom threw open the front door, jumped over the porch steps, and began running up and down the street in the pouring rain shouting, "Yeah!" with his arms waving in the air.

"He was just so excited," Norma recalled, having watched the sight from the bedroom window. "I mean, he knew I was there for good. It was such a wonderful moment. I then really believed that we would always be together."

Several days later, Norma walked down the street and got a job at Dover Footwear, one of several manufacturing businesses that had occupied the enormous, now largely abandoned, old brick linen mills that sat along the Cochecho River. Having completed her junior year, she decided to drop out of school rather than face the pressure of a new high school. "You know how it is for a teenager changing schools," she later reflected.

The rest of the summer was heaven. Tom would come over to the mill every day at lunchtime and wave up to the third floor, where Norma and her girlfriends worked. They would all wave back and shout, "Norma, Tom's here!" in a mocking sing-song tone. She would then run down the stairs, out the door, hug Tom, and spend the lunch hour sitting on the steps laughing, telling stories, and stealing the occasional kiss. They saw each other every day, made weekend trips to York Beach, ate clams, and went out for pizza and ice cream. When not working, Tom spent almost all this spare time at the Morrill house. He was quickly becoming part of the family. They all adored him.

The summer did not go smoothly at the Morrissey house, however. While having Norma in Dover was heaven for Tom, it proved to be the last straw between him and his mother. She had been steadfastly opposed to the relationship from the beginning. The Medford incident had only made matters worse. Now she felt that her authority was being openly challenged. Days before Tom was to begin began his senior year, Lorraine confronted him with an ultimatum.

"If you want to live under this roof and stay in high school, then you had better get rid of that girl. If you don't, you will be on your own. You'll have to join the military. That's your choice. The girl or your family. The decision is yours."

There was a military draft in 1965 that required all boys who had reached their eighteenth birthday to register. If they were of sound physical and mental health, the chances were good that they would have to serve at least two years in the armed forces. High school and college students were deferred until they either dropped out of school or completed four years of college. Tom had just turned seventeen, so he would not be eligible for the draft for another year. He could, however, enlist with his parents' permission. He asked his mother if they'd be willing to give it. She stood her ground and said yes but was certain that it would never come to that.

Boys from Dover had been enlisting in the military for years. The most recent local war casualty had occurred during the Korean War fifteen years earlier. Those who were shipped overseas usually went to Japan, South Korea, or West Germany for a year or two and came home. In 1965, the American troop escalation in Vietnam was just beginning. Most people assumed that the few troops who were there would be home in a year. It had likely not occurred to Tom or his mother that by enlisting he might have to fight in a war. Her one goal was to get him away from Norma.

For Tom, this was a simple choice. He loved his parents and siblings, but his future was with Norma. That evening, the two lovers talked about it late into the night. Norma cried and begged him not to enlist. She had a job. Together they would find a way to make do. They could live with her mother and sisters until he finished high school. He could continue to work after school and on weekends. They would get married after he graduated, start a family, and begin a life of their own. To her, the military was not an option if she could keep him in school.

Almost overnight, however, Tom became a man. He felt responsible for Norma and for her family. He wanted to take care of her and provide a future for them. He knew that while Norma's plan could work, he did not want to endure another long year to get on with their lives together. To him, the solution was simple and obvious. Joining the military was the only way he felt he could support the two of them and the family they were planning to have.

Several days later, with the signed permission letter from his parents folded up in his back pocket, Tom Morrissey took his mother's white station wagon, drove over to Portsmouth, and signed up for a four-year enlistment in the United States Marine Corps.

It was September 1965.

The following week, Tom, a small bag in hand, kissed and hugged Norma on the platform of the Dover station as the Boston-bound train approached. Norma tried to hold back her tears, but the changes she and Tom had endured over the previous year had already been so wrenching that she wasn't sure where she could find the room to emotionally absorb all that was now unfolding before her. She was devastated.

After arriving at Boston's North Station, Tom had made his way over to South Station, received his official orders from the local recruiter, and fell in with a dozen other recruits who would join him on the seventeen-hour journey to the Marine Corps Recruit Depot in Parris Island, South Carolina.

CHAPTER 11

Winter and spring 1970, Cambridge

The previous fall, I had joined the Owl Club, one of a dozen so-called Final Clubs on campus where undergraduates could dine, study, and socialize. Because I now lived off campus, it provided a convenient nexus for my daily college life.

Like most of Harvard's clubs at the time, The Owl, as it was known, was largely composed of privileged white males. The racial, educational, and geographic diversity that had made the Marine Corps such a rich brotherhood for me did not exist here. In retrospect, I was regressing—not to my recent Marine Corps past—but all the way back to Andover, that comfortably conservative haven that had nurtured me. I was unconsciously doing everything I could to mentally erase my time in the military. It was easier that way.

To stay productively occupied during Jayne's absence, I enrolled in a slate of challenging second-semester courses.

Given my early academic success, I thought I could handle the increased workload. I was motivated—even excited. My reward would be a planned summer of backpacking through Europe with Jayne.

The semester began well. I bought my books, attended the first several weeks of classes, and threw myself into the work. It felt good. One evening my friend, Pat Grant, invited me to go skiing with him in Vermont. He said that his family owned a place near Stratton Mountain. I thanked him, said that I didn't ski, and declined. He said he'd teach me. I told him I had no equipment. He said we'd find some—cheap. So, that weekend, the two of us headed north. We had a ball. The following weekend, we returned. We kept returning for the balance of the winter, sometimes for a week at a time.

By the time the mountain closed for the season in early April, I had missed over a month of classes and fallen so far behind that it was difficult for me to see how I could pass even one of my five courses. I became consumed with shame. I thought of my parents. I thought of the people at Andover and Harvard who had put their faith in my ability to succeed. Would I now have to stay in Cambridge this summer to make up the coursework? I thought of Jayne. I was planning to meet her in Oxford in June.

Had she been there, Jayne, a practicing Catholic, might have suggested that I pray. Religion had not played a prominent role in my life. I had gone to Sunday school growing up, and daily chapel had been required at Andover. On Parris Island, the mandatory Sunday morning services were a welcome respite from the tough grind of boot camp. I recall one Sunday when, while I was gazing around the chapel lost in a daydream, Staff Sergeant Hilton, our senior drill instructor, tapped me on the shoulder with his swagger stick and uttered the admonition, "Pray, motherfucker, pray."

"Aye, aye, sir," I whispered and dutifully lowered my head and closed my eyes.

Another year passed before I gave a second thought to religion. One evening at Camp Pendleton, days before departing for Vietnam, a padre walked through the barracks and handed me a set of rosary beads. I didn't know what they were or under what circumstances they might be used, but I figured they couldn't hurt, so I threw them into my backpack.

Nine months later, on the afternoon of June 6, 1968, the final day of the battle for LZ Loon, as a shrinking number of us were clinging to a small perimeter near the top of the hill, I fished the rosary beads out of my backpack and bowed my head. I hoped that all those years of Sunday school and chapel had earned me some positive equity.

Dear God, I began.

I've never prayed or asked you for anything before.

I now pray that you get me out of here safely and back home in one piece.

Thank you and amen.

An hour later, with the sun lowering beyond the far western ridgeline, I heard the sound to which my ears had become delicately attuned. Within minutes, the first of several evacuation helicopters landed on top of the hill, and a dozen incredulous marines scrambled aboard. We had been certain that we would never make it off LZ Loon alive. The next chopper came seconds later. Enemy mortar fire commenced. A third one swooped in, loaded up, and got out without touching the ground. Small-arms fire was coming at us from the jungle below. We had already seen two choppers shot down earlier in the day. I got aboard the fourth one. Our worst fears were not realized. Exhausted, dazed, and enormously relieved, we were deposited into the relative security of the Vandergrift Combat Base minutes later.

I then remembered my prayer and felt that words of thanks were in order.

Dear God,

Great job. Thank you.

Amen.

Now, nearly two years later, in April 1970, I was again faced with an intractable situation. While not exactly life-or-death, it was beginning to feel that way. With the arrival of spring, protests had again besieged the Harvard campus. The escalating opposition to the war in Vietnam had driven students to join what had become a nationwide movement of unimagined intensity. With my back to the academic wall, I tried to stay out of the fray. I attended classes, spent hours in the library, took brief breaks for meals, and wrote Jayne. With every passing day, however, it became increasingly clear that I couldn't make up for the time I had lost to a semester of skiing.

On May 1, President Nixon escalated the war and outraged the protesters by secretly ordering American B-52s to bomb Cambodia, South Vietnam's western neighbor. The North Vietnamese had been using neighboring Cambodia from which to conduct strikes into South Vietnam. US forces had previously been prohibited from conducting military operations in Cambodia. Several days later, on Monday, May 4, while peacefully protesting the Cambodian incursion, four students at Kent State University in Ohio were shot dead and nine others wounded by Ohio National Guardsmen. The Guard had been activated by the governor to quell what he feared was turning into a potential riot. The outrage throughout the country was profound. University administrators became understandably concerned about the safety of their students. "Remember Kent State and Cambodia" became the battle cry that further energized the protestors.

During those tumultuous days, I remained in the library, leaving only for meals, sleep, and occasional forays out to Harvard Yard to watch the screaming mob of my fellow students. Standing on the library steps looking down at the scene, I felt completely detached. Most of the protestors were undergraduates whose draft deferments were soon to expire. Many could find themselves in Vietnam in less than a year. I thought it was amusing—indeed entertaining. I wondered to myself how committed they would be had there not been a draft.

There was nothing amusing, however, about my own plight. I was disconsolate and acutely aware that I had only myself to blame. The shame that I felt was crippling. In desperation, I found a quiet corner in the library stacks, knelt, and again bowed my head. It seemed easier this time, perhaps because I felt that, after the miracle in Vietnam, God and I had developed the beginnings of a relationship.

Hi God.

It's me again.

I know ... I brought this one on myself. My life's not in danger like the last time, but I am in a tough spot.

I pray that you can do *something*, although I can't imagine what that might be.

Thank you ... again.

Amen

I returned to my cubicle, nearly alone in the emptied library, and continued the Sisyphean task of trying to master a semester's worth of work in the week that I had left. An hour later, I spotted my Owl Club friend Todd Jennings returning several books at the main counter. When he noticed me, he walked over with a bewildered look on his face.

"Jack, what are you doing here?" he asked.

It was a fair question. We had not seen each other since January. I began to tell him about my plight, but he quickly cut me off.

"President Pusey just shut down the university," he said, "because of Kent State and Cambodia. He was afraid something bad might happen here if the protests kept escalating. Anyway, the semester's over. We're supposed to leave the campus by noon tomorrow."

"Over?" I spluttered. It was unimaginable.

"Over," Todd responded with the trace of a smile.

"What about finals?" I stammered in disbelief.

"Anyone registered this semester," he replied, "gets a passing grade in all courses."

"You're shitting me," I said, stupefied. I could think of no cogent response.

"No, really," he concluded. "Have a great summer. See you in the fall."

I sat back down in stunned silence for several minutes until I was informed that the library was closing. With my books, yellow pads, pencils, and pens in hand, I headed for the exit.

Outside, Harvard Yard was eerily silent, in stark contrast to the noisy exuberance of only hours before. As I walked down the library steps, I paused, looked up and—gratefully astonished—smiled and said out loud,

Thanks, God.

You are amazing.

Amen.

Then I thought about the four students from Kent State University whose deaths had given rise to my good fortune. It was a ghastly tradeoff. I felt sick to my stomach. The killing of innocent American kids had, until now, been limited to the war in Vietnam half a world away. Now it had not only come home but arrived on a college campus like the one that I was walking across at that moment.

CHAPTER 12

Summer 1970, Europe

In late June, I boarded a packed student charter flight and flew to England. I'd been looking forward to this moment for six months. Had Jayne changed? I knew that I had and was not proud of the result. I had squandered the semester and had a romantic fling with a woman I had met while skiing. Absent Jayne, I felt as though my life had lost all direction. I desperately hoped that we could restore the magic we had once shared.

After arriving at Gatwick Airport early the next morning, I grabbed my backpack, took the Tube to Paddington Station, and boarded a train for the one-hour trip to Oxford. After taking a cab to her flat and walking up three flights of stairs, the door opened, and there stood Jayne like a vision before me. She glowed with the same radiant smile. Her dark eyes twinkled, and her straight brown hair now extended halfway down her back. In an instant, our time apart vanished. It was glorious to see her. We hugged, kissed briefly, then after standing back to look at each other, hugged again.

That evening, we met several of her friends at a local pub. I doubt that I was good company. I was jet-lagged and distracted by the warm beer, strange food, and unfamiliar faces. I was also grappling with how and when I would tell Jayne that I had been unfaithful in her absence. The next morning, we walked to a nearby cafe for breakfast. After the coffee arrived, she reached across the table for my hand and said that she had something to tell me.

"I slept with Roger last March," she began. Roger had been one of the friends who had joined us for dinner the night before. "It was just one night. I was lonely. He's my friend. I have no other feelings for him. I'm sorry. Can you possibly understand? Will you forgive me?"

The blood rushed to my head. I was overcome by a surge of jealousy. Understand? Forgive? I became angry, then quickly caught myself before responding. How could I possibly judge her given what had been my own behavior that spring?

"I do understand." I stumbled, although I didn't. The thought of her with another man rattled me to the core. "I slept with a girl in Vermont last spring." There, I said it.

Jayne thoughtfully paused, looked up into my eyes, and asked, "Do you love her?"

"No," I responded. "It was just ... well ... you know."

We continued to awkwardly talk over coffee while trying to span the chasm that had formed between us. Jayne was patient and understanding. I was largely mute and unresponsive.

Later that afternoon, we took the train into London, had dinner at a small Indian restaurant in the West End, and went to see *Hair*, the tribal love-rock musical, at the Shaftesbury Theatre. The controversial show, which had premiered two years earlier to a packed house at Broadway's Biltmore Theater, contained scenes of public nudity, recreational drug-taking, anti–Vietnam War protests, and American flag desecration. *New York Post* theater critic Richard Watts Jr. wrote, "its high spirits are contagious, and its young zestfulness makes it difficult to resist." Most theater critics agreed. Many Americans, however, did not. They felt that the production graphically illustrated the complete breakdown of American social mores that had been building throughout the 1960s. *Hair*, they said, had become a small but representative piece of the greatest level of social unrest seen in the United States since the Civil War a century earlier.

The London audience loved the show. They sang along with the music, cheered the anti–Vietnam War references and—as the overture continued after the curtain call—ran onto the stage to dance with the cast. Several people took off their clothes.

Jayne pulled me up onto the stage and encouraged me to join in the dancing. I tried to be a good sport but was stupefied by the musical's unabashed anti-Americanism. I was not naive. Having been home for nearly two years, I'd watched as colleges, including my own, had erupted in anti-war protests. This audience, however, was foreign, and the target was the

United States. At first, I felt uncomfortable. Before long the feeling morphed into anger. I wasn't mad at Jayne. She was being herself. I didn't know where I could constructively direct my bile. I was swirling helplessly in a world that felt like it was going down the drain and taking me with it.

After the show, as we walked back across the West End to the Tube, I felt consumed by the mobs of exiting theatergoers and addled by the strange smells and loud city noises. The novelty of being back with Jayne was also wearing off. I was jealous, hurt, and angry that she had not been faithful in my absence, and I was ashamed and guilt-ridden about my own behavior. Try as I might, I could not reconcile the two sets of feelings. Jayne and I had always been able to talk through whatever issues arose between us. The long separation, however, had made communication strained.

When we awoke the next morning, I was in a funk. Jayne had forgiven me and wanted only to move forward. I could not. I didn't even want to try.

"Let's get out of here," I said. "Right now. This morning." I didn't know where we would go or how we would get there, but I did not want to stay in Oxford for another hour.

Jayne did her best to lift my sagging spirits. She was encouraging—even cheerful. During her semester abroad, she'd excelled in her coursework, made new friends, and loved England. She was eager to share it all with me and determined to talk me through whatever it was that had me so frozen.

"I have two weeks left in the semester," she replied. "If you can't wait that long, will you please just tell me where you are going, and I will meet you there."

I told her that I would try but knew in my heart that I probably wouldn't. That afternoon we took the bus to Oxford station and shared a mutually uncertain goodbye. The train came, and I boarded, waved, and headed back to London. It was awful. Jayne was crying. I wanted to cry but couldn't find the tears. I sat next to a window, bent over with my head in my hands, and didn't move until we debarked at Paddington Station an hour later. Jayne and I would not see each other again until the fall.

The next day, I took a train to Edinburgh, Scotland, and hitchhiked across the country to Duart Castle on the Isle of Mull, the ancestral home of the Clan MacLean since the fifteenth century. My ancient family history oozed from every stone. My great-grandfather had been a stonemason who had emigrated from Scotland to Paterson, New Jersey, 150 years before. I was proud to be one small piece of a continuum that stretched back centuries. Had any of them been to war? I silently asked them for guidance. What had their lives been like when they returned? Why was I feeling the way I was feeling?

Over the next five weeks, I hitchhiked aimlessly around Europe, from Amsterdam to East Berlin, Munich, and Croatia. I thought about Jayne, wondered where she was, and who she was traveling with, but the more distance and time that separated me from Oxford, the more her memory faded. I did wonder what would happen when we got back to Boston in the fall, but not with any great anticipation.

With my trip nearing its end, I hitched back across Europe to Munich, where I treated myself to an eight-hour train ride to Paris, the departure point for my charter flight home. My first stop after arriving was the American Express office. It was common at the time for traveling students to have our mail sent to the local office to be held for our arrival. Having ditched my original itinerary when I left for Berlin, Paris was my first mail stop in over a month. I had several letters. One was from Jayne, telling me about her summer travels through Spain and France and expressing concern that I had been out of touch. The others were from my mother, filling me in on family news and urging me to write.

Days later, when I stepped off the plane in Boston, my appearance was in stark contrast to what it had been when I left. With shoulder-length hair and a shaggy beard, I was wearing leather pants, sandals, and a cotton pullover shirt with a bright-red Mao pin attached. That I was immediately pulled aside at the customs counter should not, in retrospect, have been a surprise.

CHAPTER 13

October 1966, Dover

Boot camp was rigorous, but Tom endured—even excelled—despite being the youngest boy in the platoon. At the conclusion, he and the balance of his company boarded the buses that took them three hours north to Camp Geiger on the Marine Corps base at Camp Lejeune, North Carolina. There they would receive a month of advanced infantry training and, for the first time, be treated like United States Marines.

At the conclusion of infantry training—fourteen weeks after their arrival on Parris Island—the freshly minted marines were granted a thirty-day leave. Now a seventeen-year-old Marine Corps private, Tom Morrissey was desperate to get home to Norma. On the Friday afternoon that his leave began, Tom grabbed his seabag from the barracks, found his way to the on-base carpool staging area, paid five dollars to a northbound driver, squeezed himself in with a carload of other marines, and departed for New York City. It was the first leg of his journey home to Dover. Stops were made only for gas.

Nine hours later, after passing through the Lincoln Tunnel and entering Midtown Manhattan, the driver deposited his carload of young marines on the sidewalk in front of the Terminal Bar at the corner of Eighth Avenue and Forty-First Street. The bar, which sat directly across Eighth Avenue from the Port Authority Bus Terminal, was home to drifters, hookers, pimps, drug addicts, transvestites, and the occasional Irish mob boss. It had, over the years, established a well-earned reputation as the "rowdiest bar in New York City."

Twice a week, every week, on Saturday after midnight and late Sunday afternoon, this witches' brew of human detritus was joined by a cadre of itinerate well-scrubbed young United States Marines. For some, it became the site of their first legal drink, for others, their introduction to illicit sex. For all Northeastern boys serving in the military in the 1960s, it was the way station between the massive military bases in the Southeastern United States and home, sitting as it did at the center of one of the world's most efficient transportation hubs. For a generation of marines, the sidewalk in front of the Terminal Bar existed as the transfer station for those who needed rides and those who might provide them.

After he arrived, Tom sought out another driver who was headed to northern New England. Even at this hour, the cars were pouring in, and the sidewalk in front of the Terminal Bar was crowded with transient military enlisted men awaiting their next carpool connection. After a brief wait, Tom found a driver going to New Hampshire, gave him five dollars, hopped in, and began the five-hour drive home to Norma. Thirty days later, at the conclusion of his leave, he reversed the process by hitching a ride back to the Terminal Bar, piling into a car with Lejeune-bound marines, and driving nine hours back to base.

For the next twenty months, while serving as a military policeman stationed at Camp Lejeune and later at Naval Station Norfolk, Virginia, Tom never failed to get home to Norma almost every weekend. To do so, he'd either get a hop on a military plane to New Hampshire's Pease Air Force Base or make the Friday drive north via the Terminal Bar. Most liberty calls were for forty-eight hours. Perhaps once a month, with good behavior and an understanding sergeant, it could be extended to seventy-two hours. But for the occasional weekend lost to mandatory guard duty, Morrissey never once failed to get home. With Norma on the receiving end, his weekly treks were neither exhausting nor routine. He was young, strong, employed, madly in love, and starting a family. That he was making any kind of personal sacrifice never occurred to him. His adult life was dawning in spectacular fashion.

Underlying the joy that they felt during that time was America's increasing combat presence in Vietnam. At the start of 1965, the year of Tom's enlistment, there were about 23,000 American troops in Vietnam. By the end of the following year, the number had spiked to nearly 400,000. Most were United States Marines. It was now becoming increasingly clear that, with over two years left in his enlistment, the odds that Tom might be sent to Vietnam were growing by the day.

Throughout that winter and into the spring and summer, Norma continued to live with her mother and sisters on Park Street and work first shift at Dover Footwear. Tom continued to come home on weekends and, while he might stop by to look in on his family, he stayed with Norma. Tom's mother, Lorraine, who had despised Norma from the start, now felt that she was responsible for Tom's dropping out of school, enlisting in the Marine Corps, and leaving home. Norma did not join Tom on his visits home. In deference to their mother, Tom's seven siblings largely ignored her as well.

That fall, Norma and Tom decided to get married. After revealing their plans to Tom's aunt Mickey, she drove them over to Concord to get their blood tests. A week later, they presented themselves at the Dover Municipal Building, got a marriage license and, several days after that, with little fanfare, were married by a justice of the peace on Mount Vernon Street. Norma's mother and sisters were there as well as Aunt Mickey and several friends. While they were invited, at Lorraine's direction, there were no members of Tom's immediate family in attendance.

It was a glorious moment; the happiest day they could possibly imagine. All that was in the past was over. They would, at last, have their lives to themselves. It was the beginning of something great. After supper at the local pizza shop, they walked across the street to the Dover Municipal Building and attended the monthly community dance, with Norma still in her wedding dress. They danced, they hugged, they laughed, and Norma showed off her wedding ring to everybody who came by.

It was October 29, 1966. Norma was three months pregnant.

CHAPTER 14

Winter/Spring 1971, Cambridge

Jayne returned to Boston to begin her senior year shortly after I got back. I'd hoped that our return to familiar surroundings might rekindle that which had been lost, but the pieces never fell into place. I pushed her away without providing an explanation. It was confusing to me and hurtful to her.

Home again, the nightmares returned, and without Jayne, I again became daunted by feelings of loneliness and depression. The graphic, inescapable reminders of the ongoing war were again spread across the front pages of the morning newspapers and broadcast on the television evening news. While the summer had given me a six-week respite from Vietnam, the haunting memories had again become a painful preoccupation. I didn't want to be in Cambridge, and I didn't want to be in college. For that matter, there was no place I could conjure that I might want to be.

I gave brief thought to driving back up to New Hampshire to find Norma. Her son would now be four years old. Was she suffering? Perhaps our shared love of Tom would bring us both some solace. I could think of no one else within driving range who had shared, albeit indirectly, that horrifying day when he was killed. But I didn't have a car, didn't know if she still lived there, and … I always found it easier to come up with reasons not to go.

I began my junior year inside of this shell. I couldn't escape the past and still had no idea about what I might productively do with my future. Given the near-disaster of the previous spring, however, I did want to prove to myself that I could compete academically. I shaved, cut my hair, dropped my flirtation with Mao, and enrolled in a Chinese history course. I was ready to go forward with renewed vigor.

That fall, the Owl Club became an integral part of my daily college life. I rode my bike over from Somerville first thing in the morning, had coffee, read the daily newspapers, walked back and forth to classes, ate lunch, and studied there in the afternoon. During idle moments, I watched TV, played back-gammon, and developed new friendships. Several of my fellow members had been friends from Andover. The Owl was com-fortably familiar—an easy place to slide into. I did not feel judged. I felt accepted.

As I spent more time at the Owl, I spent less time thinking about Loon. When my mind did drift back to Vietnam, I dis-tracted myself by playing small-stakes games of backgammon.

This seemed to work, for a while, anyway. By the midway point of the fall semester, however, the idle distraction grew into an obsession. My occasional fifteen-minute games morphed into half-day or all-night marathons. The small stakes grew, and the action became more intense. While playing backgammon, I became enveloped by a mesmerizing fog. I thought of nothing beyond the game board. I also began to drink more heavily. I was looking for something—anything—to replace the adrenaline surges that had been so intoxicating and addictive in Vietnam. I was also trying to forget. Backgammon and alcohol helped me achieve both.

In January, at the end of the first semester of my junior year, I met Roz Kemper, a second-grade teacher at a private day school in Brookline. Roz was a breath of fresh air. She was lovely, smart, funny, and responsible, and became a delightful addition to my stagnating life. Our courtship was calm and manageable, with little of the intensity or drama that had defined my relationship with Jayne. Her father was a West Point graduate. She admired my Marine Corps service and was proud that I had served in Vietnam. She worked during the week, I studied, and we found time to be together on weekends. As we fell in love, my mood swings began to stabilize. I was determined to bring structure and self-discipline back into my life. I knew from recent experience that I was unlikely to do so by myself.

Jayne was back across the river, finishing her senior year at Boston University. I had seen her once that fall after our return from Europe but had since shut her out of my life. One winter afternoon, John O'Day, the club steward, found me at the gaming table and asked that I come back into the kitchen. There, sitting on the counter, was a beautiful wooden cage that contained two chirping lovebirds. I silently looked over to him for guidance.

"A girl named Jayne dropped this off and asked that I give it to you," he said.

I had no words. I was dumbfounded. I had boxed her out of my life for six months for reasons that I could not articulate. Now she had returned with this loving, thoughtful offering. It was pure Jayne. In an instant, my feelings for her rushed back into the void. I still loved her. I wanted to apologize. I wanted to tell her what a shit I'd been. I wanted to be with her now. I wanted to spend my life with her. For that moment, the rest of my world evaporated, and there was only Jayne.

But there wasn't only Jayne. There was Roz. We were several months into a burgeoning relationship. I'd told her that Jayne was out of my life, which I thought was true. As John reached to hand me the cage, I froze. My life since Jayne had been teetering on the edge. Thanks to Roz, I felt that it was coming back together. I didn't want to hurt her. I felt that my sanity depended on it.

"No," I said to John, "I don't want the birds." I walked out of the kitchen and back to the gaming table.

"What am I going to do with them?" John asked, following behind me.

I stopped, turned, and said, "I don't care, John. Keep them. Give them back to her. I don't care."

I don't know what became of the birds. Perhaps Jayne came back and got them. Maybe John kept them. Either way, I never saw them again.

In early June, having completed my junior year, Roz and I drove down to Long Island to attend a friend's wedding. It was a relief to get away from Cambridge. We were looking forward to a fun weekend with friends in the lovely town of Cold Spring Harbor. We would be staying nearby in Northport with my mother's sister Barbara and her family. It was familiar territory for me. My family had lived in Northport when I was born and, ever since, return visits to the town to see my cousins had been special occasions.

On Friday evening, we attended the rehearsal dinner with the rest of the wedding party. The groom had transferred to Harvard the previous year, having served with the Green Berets in Vietnam. While we felt a strong bond, we rarely spoke about our shared experience. This evening, unlike the many that we had spent in combat, was a happy one. There were lots of toasts, many jokes, and the dinner lasted well into the night. He was beginning a promising new post-Vietnam life. Perhaps soon, I would too. I was beginning to think that it was possible,

The following morning, I got up, brushed my teeth, and dragged myself into the shower. As I emerged, Roz was standing outside of the bathroom door.

"Jack," she began, "your mother just called." After a pause, she continued. "She called with bad news. Jayne's dead. She was killed in an automobile accident in England earlier this week." She paused again. "I am so sorry."

I stood there, without comment, waiting for her to continue. Jayne dead?

"Her family has been trying to find you for several days," she continued. "The funeral is Monday. They hope you will attend."

Several weeks earlier, after her graduation, Jayne had returned to England. She was twenty-one years old. The news was devastating. I went into the bedroom, sat down, hung my head, and thought that I would cry, but I couldn't. No matter how hard I tried, even this terrible news could not evoke a single tear. Had I lost all feeling?

The next day, Roz drove back to Boston, and I took a train into New York. There I met several of Jayne's friends who were driving to Bethlehem, Pennsylvania, for the funeral Mass. Since hearing the news, my mind had been a conflicting blur of wonderful memories and deep remorse. The two emotions tugged hard at each other. Remorse was, however, the easy victor. I believed that by having known and loved her, I was responsible for her death. I was twenty-four years old, and the people I loved were still being killed.

The funeral Mass was held with an open casket before the altar. Two acoustic guitar players strummed a musical rendition of "I am the resurrection and the light, he who believes in me will never ever die" from John 11:25. Row by row, the attendees rose and walked up to view her. Jayne's father, mother, three sisters, and several relatives sat in the front pew as the mourners filed by. Most nodded to them in silent acknowledgment. Several stepped over and offered a quiet whisper of condolence. When my turn came to pass, I could do neither. I looked down and saw yet another young dead body. Jayne wasn't splayed on a remote Vietnam hillside, however. She was in quiet repose in a lovely church in Bethlehem. She looked beautiful. Her Martin guitar lay in the coffin beside her.

After the service, the Budura family invited the attendees to their home for a small gathering. I didn't want to go but knew that I had to. It had been easy for me to back out of paying my respects to the Morrissey family on my abortive trip to Dover three years earlier. They didn't know me and hadn't known that I might be coming. This was different. I knew her parents and her three sisters. As awkwardly as our relationship had ended, they had asked me to come, so I wanted to give what little comfort my presence might bring.

I spotted Jayne's mother as soon as I walked into their home. She was speaking with several people on the far side of the living room. When she saw me, she stopped talking, turned, and walked purposefully in my direction. We instinctively held out our hands, shared a kiss on the cheek, and looked back at each other in silence.

"I'm so glad that you were able to come," she said. "It took us two days to find out how to get a hold of you. It is so important to all of us that you are here."

"Thank you," I replied. "Thank you for letting me know. Thank you for asking me to come. I am so sorry, Dot. So sorry." The tears welled but didn't come. Hers flowed freely.

I felt overwhelmed, not only with grief but with guilt and shame. Despite having been absent from their lives for well over a year, her mother and sisters—as devastatingly sad as they certainly were—seemed glad to see me. They introduced me to the gathered mourners as though I were a member of the family.

But I was in shock. After our initial greeting, although we spoke for several minutes, I could not bear to look her mother in the eyes. I did share brief words with her father, hugged each of her sisters, and said hello to several of the extended family members and friends who were present. I barely recall speaking a coherent sentence to anyone I met that afternoon. While the responsibility for her death weighed heavily on my shoulders, I had lost my ability to grieve during the afternoon of June 5, 1968, when Tom Morrissey and seven other boys were killed within minutes during a blistering rocket attack. Had I been killed, Jayne would still be alive. Had I not been such a shit to her during the past year, Jayne would still be alive. While the guilt that I felt from her death weighed heavily on my shoulders, my capacity for self-reproach had become limitless.

I returned to Somerville late that night, collapsed on my bed, and blankly stared up at the ceiling until dawn.

Mostly I thought about the birdcage.

CHAPTER 15

1972, Cambridge and New York

That summer, I got a job working at the Harvard University Information Office, which continued through my senior year. I conducted campus tours, gave directions, and answered questions from tourists, prospective students, and their families.

Roz and I continued to see each other through the summer and fall. As we fell in love, we talked about what our lives might be like after graduation. My weekdays were spent attending classes, studying, playing backgammon, and sitting alone at home drinking beer well into the night. During the weekends, I worked at the Information Office and saw Roz. They were the two positives that I knew were keeping me sane. I clung to them dearly.

Roz and I became engaged in December and planned a summer wedding. The engagement went well for several months. We decided on a small wedding with family and friends. We looked at china patterns, kitchen utensils, and furniture. It was a novel feeling to share life decisions. I liked it. I was happy. I loved Roz. We enjoyed spending time together. Our friends and families were thrilled. I began to ponder what I'd do after graduation now that there would be two of us to think about.

Late one winter night, as occasionally happened, I recalled a moment on Loon. During the intense firefight on June 6, we were being shot at by a sniper on an adjacent hillside. He had already hit several of us. Larry Price, the company's rocket man, and I slid out of our adjacent holes, lay prone in the open, and gingerly assembled a 3.5-inch rocket launcher. The "Bazooka," as it was known, was a notoriously unreliable World War II vintage antitank weapon that had somehow survived passage into the modern Marine Corps. Larry sighted the weapon as I loaded a round. The sniper spotted us and fired two rounds in our direction. The first cracked over our heads. The second slammed into the dirt in front of us. On the upside, he was a lousy shot. On the downside, he had us bracketed.

Larry whispered "clear," the signal that he was about to fire. I lay flat and held my ears. He pulled the trigger. Nothing. "Clear." He pulled the trigger again. Nothing. I sat up, removed the round, licked the bottom, rubbed it hard against my shirt, and reinserted it. "Clear." Still nothing. Frustrated, we abandoned the weapon and scampered back into the safety of our holes.

I'd previously emptied an eighteen-round magazine in the direction of the sniper to no effect. Now, having seen the muzzle blasts from the two rounds that he had fired at us, we had a better idea of his exact location. I grabbed my rifle, inserted a fresh magazine, took careful aim, and waited for him to appear. I had no other place that I had to be. Five minutes passed before I saw the top of his head emerge from the parapet. I took a breath, slowly exhaled, and gently squeezed off two rounds. The second one appeared to hit him in the left shoulder as he spun around and disappeared.

I wondered if he had survived my shot. I wondered how old he was. Like me, he probably had parents and siblings who worried about him every day. Then, sitting alone in the basement, I'd wonder what would have happened to me if his first shot had been a few inches lower or if his second shot had been a few inches higher. I'd be dead, and Jayne would be alive. Would only that he had been a better shot, I thought.

Roz and I had talked little about Vietnam. She knew that I didn't want to talk about it, so she didn't press. Many of these vivid random memories continued to demand space in my brain, however. I had no control over when they'd come or how I'd react when they did. I didn't want to share them with Roz. I could see no benefit to either of us by dragging her into the darkness of my military memories. I continued to be grasped by the stranglehold of my past. I wasn't ready to move on at all.

In early March, I began to get cold feet. Instead of anticipating our new life together, I worried about losing my old life, although there was little about it that I thought I'd miss. Still, there were unfinished issues that lingered. I was still drinking, I was still gambling, and I was still haunted by Vietnam. In what had become a familiar turn of my emotions, I began to detach from Roz, much as I had from Jayne. We stopped seeing each other on weekends, and soon I stopped calling her as well. I offered no explanation. Later in the spring, she returned the engagement ring to my mother in Brookline, who was equally baffled by my behavior.

An academic highlight of that spring was a course on presidential power, taught by a young, rosy-cheeked redhead named Doris Kearns. Professor Kearns had recently returned from several months at the LBJ Ranch in Texas, where she had been researching her first book, *Lyndon Johnson and the American Dream*. Totally engaging, she regaled us with riveting stories that brought LBJ's tempestuous six-year tenure into sharp historical and human focus. While I had once admired LBJ for his early legislative success in the areas of civil rights, social welfare, and wilderness preservation, I had since come to despise him for his reckless escalation of the war that had killed so many of my comrades in arms.

It had now been nearly four years since my return. While Johnson had been out of office for most of that time, the Vietnam War was still raging. Professor Kearns, armed with historical perspective, was able to thoughtfully provide us with a rare look into the soul of this larger-than-life figure who, she said, would have been a worthy protagonist in any Shakespearean tragedy. My opinion of the man was tempered as I began to better understand the potential for good and evil that resides within all of us. Presidents, she often noted, were still human beings. For better and often for worse, however, the impact of their every decision may be magnified a thousand-fold. One morning, perhaps to reinforce the fact that most of these decisions are not made in a vacuum, she noted that much of the advice that LBJ had received about the war's conduct had come from former and existing Harvard professors, who had stood at the very lectern that she now occupied. Author David Halberstam had called them, "The Best and the Brightest" in his book of the same name. It wasn't a compliment.

I graduated that spring with a bachelor's degree in American history. Having now been the fortunate recipient of an outstanding education and an honorable discharge from the United States Marine Corps, I felt confident that somebody would want to hire me. I made a snap decision to move to New York, which I thought would be a good place to begin my professional career. I didn't own a decent suit or dress shirt. The only presentable shoes I owned were my ill-fitting spit-polished Marine Corps–issued dress shoes. I took what little money I had, ventured downtown to Filene's Basement, and created a business wardrobe that would at least get me through the interview process. I also got a haircut for the first time in over a year.

After several weeks of searching, I was hired by Brown Brothers Harriman & Co., the oldest private bank in the

United States. My new boss and several of the senior staff were Andover graduates. Like the Owl Club, it felt comfortably familiar. I knew little about banking, but they had a training program that would get me started and provide the structure I knew I needed. Going forward, my life could only improve.

When I returned to my parents' home in Brookline, there was a letter from Roz, inviting me to join her for the weekend at her family's summer cottage in Maine. It was an olive branch that came with no underlying expectations. I still had feelings for Roz and felt badly about the way I had treated her that spring. I accepted the invitation.

The moment I spotted her at the Portland Jetport, my love for Roz flooded back and overcame the past fears and lingering guilt I had harbored. That afternoon, I asked her if she'd take me back. Her first reaction was to laugh out loud. As I persisted, however, she listened more intently. I had graduated, found a job, was moving to New York, and wanted her to join me. After several days of pleading, she relented. We were married by a justice of the peace in Brookline five days later and moved into a one-bedroom apartment in Brooklyn Heights later that month. Roz got a job teaching at a local school, and I took the subway under the East River to Wall Street every day. Our new life was beginning in a most agreeable fashion.

The Vietnam War, while winding down, remained in the news and would continue its recurring assault on my psyche for another four years. The reminders were as present as the daily newspaper headlines that I saw each morning as I emerged from the subway and the combat action reports that continued to lead the television evening news programs.

In the spring of 1973, Vietnam was pushed off the front page by the growing criminal conspiracy investigation of Vice President Spiro T. Agnew. He pleaded no contest to the charges and was forced from office the following October. This was quickly followed that spring by the rapidly developing Watergate scandal. The subsequent investigation and revelations about a possible coverup made for riveting TV viewing, as the probe increasingly focused on Nixon himself. It reached its apex during the summer of 1974, when the House Judiciary Committee passed three articles of impeachment. Rather than face the charges, President Nixon resigned from office on August 9, 1974. He was the first American president to do so.

I had voted for Nixon with the hope that a political change could get us out of Vietnam. The press said that Richard Nixon had a "secret plan" to end the war. His opponent, Senator Hubert Humphrey, as far as I could discern, had no plan at all. Now, six years later, the two most recent commanders-in-chief of the United States military—Lyndon Johnson and Richard Nixon—had quit, and the war was *still* going on.

As a result, like much of a disillusioned America, I would never again place the same level of trust in our elected officials as I had prior to Vietnam and Watergate.

CHAPTER 16

1973–1974, New York

Working at the bank revealed to me and others that I had a low tolerance for authority. This surprised me, since it had not been an issue in the Marine Corps, where I had executed direct orders well. The bank was different. I didn't like being told what to do and had thin skin for accepting criticism. My colleagues in the training program were able to turn the other cheek. I, on the other hand, pushed back against the authority. This was not a recipe for success.

I began to hear whispers that I was a volatile Vietnam veteran—a walking time bomb who was wired to blow at any time. I was aware that I could be flip and uncooperative at times but felt far from volatile. There were times, however, when I did feel anger boiling up from deep within me. My boss, not a veteran, occasionally called me "baby killer." He thought it was funny. I let it ride. I needed the job. Prior generations had proudly served and earned the country's respect, but times had changed. Many employers did not hold Vietnam veterans—particularly enlisted Vietnam veterans—in the same high regard as those who had fought in earlier wars. I later came to understand that through my behavior, I was likely transferring my anger at the way our country was treating us back to my superiors at the bank. They provided a target-rich environment.

After eighteen months, I decided to find another job.

In a fortuitous turn of events, I landed a position as the assistant ticket manager of the New York Mets. I'd always loved baseball and felt that I would never tire of a business in which my sports heroes were always nearby. The position put me in charge of season and "priority" tickets (the good seats). Many of my new colleagues were interesting characters who had worked for the Mets since the team's inception in 1962. I enjoyed listening to their stories.

The job took some learning, but I enjoyed the work and did well. During the season, all manner of people wandered into my office looking for tickets. These included the players and coaches, front-office staff, umpires, visiting team road secretaries, season ticket holders, and the unfortunate fan who had had a mustard-laden hot dog dumped on him from the upper deck. I had a small refrigerator that the concessionaire kept stocked with Schaefer beer. Visitors routinely lingered and told stories about how it used to be. For a lifelong fan, it was heaven. Yogi Berra was our manager. Tom Seaver was our ace pitcher. I got great seats for my friends. The contrast to working at the bank was striking. Most of the employees were from nearby working-class Queens. While they openly teased me about my Harvard education, they quietly respected my Vietnam service. No one ever joked about that.

After three years with the Mets, my positive attitude diminished. Several of the people whose company I had so enjoyed began to irritate me. I was told by my boss that I had developed "an attitude" and had "anger issues." I knew that something wasn't right with me, but I had no idea what it was. As I brought this workday angst home with me, Roz became concerned about my mental health, our marriage, and my job. She arranged for us to meet with a marriage counselor, with the hope that he might bring us some resolution. I told him that, at work and at home, each of my days was running into the next without resolution. This left the door open to recurring bouts of depression. I didn't understand their source and felt guilty when they came, because I knew that they were having a negative impact on Roz and on our marriage.

In 1968, when Vietnam veterans began to return home en masse, we brought with us graver physical injuries than combatants from prior wars. This was largely due to improved medical treatment in the field and the availability of hasty helicopter evacuations to first-rate medical facilities. We also brought home mental issues that would continue to haunt many of us for decades. From early on, it was suspected that Vietnam veterans were suffering from higher rates of depression, homelessness, and suicide than the rest of the country. The label "Post-Vietnam Syndrome" was used to describe the symptoms and causes of the unconsummated grief that haunted many of the returnees.

As far as I was concerned, however, I'd returned from the war whole. Ailments like Post-Vietnam Syndrome were what happened to other people. It never occurred to me until years later that I had, in fact, been mentally traumatized by the experience and symptomatically suffering from the effects since the day I got home.

Known as shell shock during World War I and combat fatigue in World War II, combatant mental issues date to the beginning of warfare. It had long been recognized that the stresses of war could cause men to break down. This was thought to be a temporary condition, brought on by overexposure to heavy combat. Given proper rest and temporary removal from the front lines, it was believed, full recovery would ensue. Those with severe cases were commonly treated with shock therapies and, in some cases, lobotomies.

The failure of many Vietnam veterans to quickly recover was initially viewed as a sign of weakness and lack of character. Because of this attitude, most veterans of our earlier wars were not sympathetic to the claims of Vietnam veterans whose symptoms might go on for months, years, and even decades. They argued that they too had experienced shell shock and combat fatigue in their wars and they'd come out of it okay.

They had *not*, in fact, come out of "it" okay at all. According to the PBS series *A Perilous Fight*, "One million three hundred ninety-three thousand soldiers were treated for 'battle fatigue' during WWII. Of all ground combat troops who fought in that war, thirty-seven percent were discharged for psychiatric reasons."

But the Vietnam War *had* been different. The United States entered World War II after being attacked on our own soil by the Japanese. Four years in duration, the war was fought for a worthy purpose and had a positive outcome. Most able-bodied Americans served, and those at home sacrificed greatly to support the war effort. The war's veterans came home by ship with their units, victorious, proud, and empowered. The shared victory was celebrated with parades in cities and towns across the country.

Our entrance into Vietnam, on the other hand, was predicated on a lie and fought with undefined goals. We had intervened in a civil war, attacked them on their soil, and never gained the national commitment to win. Over a decade in duration, few people back home sacrificed anything to the war effort, and, in the end, nobody wanted to share in the defeat. Vietnam veterans were not, consequently, considered to be parade-worthy. While much of the blame for the loss was rightfully placed on the shoulders of our national leaders—Presidents Johnson and Nixon, US Army General William Westmorland, and Secretary of Defense Robert McNamara in particular—it was the Vietnam veterans who often bore the shame. Because we had *fought* the war, we were identified *as* the war.

In 1980, the American Psychiatric Association, the arbiter of standards on mental-health diagnoses, finally recognized posttraumatic stress disorder (PTSD) as a legitimate mental ailment when it appeared for the first time in the *Diagnostic and Statistical Manual of Mental Health (DSM-III)*. Only then was it acknowledged that PTSD was cause-based and could be tied to the severe trauma experienced by healthy people. The Veterans Administration, whose psychologists and psychiatrists were charged with diagnosing and treating veterans who were suffering from the effects of PTSD could not, thereby, prior to 1980, provide the diagnosis since, according to the APA, no such ailment existed.

PTSD afflicted all of us and often impacted our families in ways we neither noticed nor understood. They were as befuddled by our behavior as we were. What all did agree on, however, was that the boy who went off to fight the war in Vietnam was different than the one who returned a year later—usually not in a good way.

Senator Alan Cranston (D-CA), a World War II veteran and an opponent of the Vietnam War, became an early advocate for developing modern treatment methods for returning Vietnam veterans. In the absence of any legislative help from Congressman Olin Teague's House Veterans Affairs Committee, Cranston initiated Senate hearings on the subject in late 1969. After the hearings and over the next four congressional sessions—an eight-year time span—Senator Cranston continued to introduce legislation that would provide for Vietnam veterans readjustment counseling. Not only did the legislation not pass, but it was also vigorously opposed by the

American Legion, VFW, and the Disabled American Veterans and rarely made it out of committee. The political power both in Congress and in the Veterans Service Organizations had long been held by Word War II and Korean War veterans. The first Vietnam veteran, John Murtha of Pennsylvania, was not elected until 1974.

The political landscape for Vietnam veterans began to change in earnest in 1977 with the election of President Jimmy Carter. A US Navy veteran, Carter supported government action to address the medical and psychological needs of Vietnam veterans. He began by appointing Georgia State Senator Max Cleland to be the first Vietnam veteran to lead the Veterans Administration. Cleland made readjustment counseling his top priority.

With the support of the new president, Cleland and Senator Cranston, now chairman of the Senate Veterans Affairs Committee, went to work to create the Vietnam Veterans Outreach Program. A key to the program's success would be the establishment of so-called Vet Centers throughout the country—places where vets could gather and receive social, psychological, and professional counseling and treatment. Over the opposition of most VSOs, the bill finally passed through Congress and was signed into law by President Carter on July 13, 1979. It was an enormous first step.

Cleland and Cranston knew that for the Vet Centers to be effective, they had to be appealing enough for Vietnam veterans to go inside. This would be a tall order since, by then, most

Vietnam veterans held the VA in low esteem. They perceived it as a place that catered primarily to the previous generation of combatants and had little interest in addressing our physical or emotional issues. Cleland and Cranston envisioned a series of urban and suburban shopping mall storefronts to be modeled after the street clinics that had sprung up in San Francisco during the 1960s. They felt it critical that, inside and out, there be no visual identifiers of a clinic's relationship with the VA or the federal government, since any Vietnam veteran who approached a Center and caught even a whiff of government involvement would never go near the place.

As the number of Vet Centers increased across the country, I began to hear positive reports about them from fellow vets. They said that there were counselors who listened, understood, and were empathetic. Many of them were Vietnam veterans themselves and had been trained to deal with the returnees. They talked about the camaraderie that was developing—how they could go in, hang out, and speak with other vets. The Centers organized group and individual readjustment sessions and provided free information and counseling regarding PTSD and Agent Orange, well before the VA acknowledged the existence of either. The Vet Centers were providing a desperately needed service and doing so extremely well. As of 2023 there are two hundred such centers across the country, offering readjustment counseling to all returning combat and noncombat veterans and their families.

Cleland, who went on to become a United States Senator from

Georgia, has often said that the Vet Center legislation was the greatest accomplishment of his decades of distinguished public service.

I never went into a Vet Center until years later. I didn't think that I needed any readjustment counseling and wasn't interested in hanging around with other vets. As far as I was concerned, I still thought that there was nothing wrong with me that had anything to do with my service in Vietnam.

It was a missed opportunity. I could not possibly have been more wrong.

CHAPTER 17

1967, Dover

The next several months, through the holidays and into the winter, became routine, but for Norma's pregnancy. She worked the first shift and Tom, now a military policeman in Norfolk, was able to make more frequent weekend trips by plane on a military hop, which added vital hours to their precious time together. With her salary and what Tom was now making after his recent promotion to lance corporal, they were more than making ends meet. They started thinking about getting their own place in Dover to live until, sometime after the baby was born, Tom could bring his young family down to live in base housing in Norfolk.

The only dark spot continued to be Tom's mother, Lorraine. When Tom was absent during the week, she badgered and harassed Norma relentlessly. She was furious when she found out about the wedding and unsuccessfully worked her contacts both in the Catholic church and the City of Dover, to have the union annulled. Shortly thereafter, when she learned that Norma was pregnant, she sent her husband down to the Morrill house with a fistful of cash to demand that she obtain an abortion. Tom was furious when he found out. While he was home on leave, he could keep his mother at bay, but in his absence, Norma could not.

Thomas J. Morrissey III was born on April 30, 1967, at the Wentworth-Douglas Hospital in Dover. Norma and Tom were overjoyed. The Morrills were also thrilled, although the addition of the baby would provide added stress to the already-crowded Park Street apartment. Together they made it work. Norma's mother and sisters helped by taking care of Thomas during the evenings, while Norma, to accommodate their schedules, switched to the second shift at Dover Footwear. Despite her aversion to Lorraine, Norma did allow her to occasionally take the baby for an afternoon or evening. She thought it was the right thing to do, since Lorraine was the child's grandmother.

Two months later, Tom and Norma rented an apartment nearby on the second floor of a three-decker house. They could afford the rent, provide for the baby, and even put a little aside every month for the coming day when they would make the move to base housing in Norfolk. That summer, they decorated and furnished the apartment, helped Norma's mother with household chores, and doted on her sisters. But for the deteriorating climate up at his family's house, Tom loved his life.

Norma had had a good relationship with Tom's seven siblings, particularly his older brother George. George was Tom's only full biological sibling. Having been adopted as infants, it's likely that Tom never knew this. Neither boy had been told by their mother. George, now twenty-one years old, had recently announced that he was gay, which was a shock to his parents. Lorraine demanded that he too move out of the house, since she felt that his continued presence would be a bad influence on the younger children. Over time, Lorraine's ongoing opposition to Norma and Tom's relationship began to wear on the rest of the family. They'd visit on the weekends when Tom was home but otherwise had little contact with Norma or the baby.

Then, in August, it happened. While leaving for home one weekend, Tom received his official orders. He was to leave for Vietnam in October. That the orders finally arrived was not a complete surprise. What had been a long shot at the time of his enlistment two years before was now a reality. American troop levels in Vietnam had been increasing by enormous numbers. They needed everybody they could get.

I got my orders to go to Vietnam a month later.

The marines had landed near Da Nang, a large port city in central South Vietnam, in March 1965, as part of President Johnson's initial escalation of the war. Prior to that, the American presence had been limited to military advisors. Tom Morrissey had enlisted in the fall of that year. By January, there were 70,000 Marines serving in Vietnam. When Tom and I got our orders, nearly two years later, the total number of American troops in Vietnam exceeded 450,000. That number rose to 536,000 the following June when he was killed.

Vietnam, a temporary global flashpoint at the time of Tom's enlistment, had grown into a real war with no end in sight.

In late August, Tom came home for the final time during a five-day travel allowance that he was granted to get from Norfolk to Camp Pendleton, California. He went up to Lexington Street alone to say goodbye to his parents and siblings. He then returned to the Hill Street apartment for a final farewell to Norma and Thomas III, by then barely five months old. It was a wrenching moment. Norma had just turned twenty years old. She was numb. Too numb to even cry for fear of unduly upsetting her son.

All marines headed to Vietnam were required to report for two weeks of staging at Camp Pendleton, California, where we received a final tune-up in jungle-combat tactics, weapons training, and administrative mechanics. ("Be sure the next of kin is up to date on your life insurance, Marine.") After the last day, we were bused up to the Marine Corps Air Station in El Toro, loaded onto a Pan Am 707, and flown to Danang.

When Tom descended the ramp into the steamy afternoon sun, he was directed to a C-130 that would take him to Charlie Company in Phu Bai. Looking out, he could see miles of rice paddies and the occasional small village. There were high, hazy hills well in the distance to the west. From afar, he thought they bore a vague resemblance to the foothills of the majestic White Mountains of New Hampshire. *Those must be the Highlands*, he thought. Several of his instructors at Camp Pendleton's Staging Battalion had been veterans of some fierce fighting in the Highlands. It would be eight months before Tom saw the Highlands again. As the plane rose higher, he could make out the blue of the South China Sea to the east.

One month later, I followed in his footsteps.

After landing in Phu Bai, Tom and several other new guys were driven in the back of an open truck to Camp Evans, several miles to the north. Evans was, at the time, the rear base for his new unit, Charlie Company, First Battalion, Fourth Marines, Third Marine Division. He used to enjoy telling us the story of his first meeting with the company gunnery sergeant.

"Welcome to Vietnam, Corporal," the gunny said while examining his orders. "Where you from?"

"New Hampshire," Tom replied.

"Never been there," the gunny said. "You ever fire an M-60 machine gun?"

"Yeah," Tom replied. "Once in infantry training and once in staging."

"Well, congratulations, Corporal," the Gunny closed. "You are the new machine gunner for the second platoon. Go over to the armory tent and draw your weapons. You'll need the M-60, an M-16 rifle, and a Colt .45 pistol."

That night, after his new platoon had safely returned from its day in the bush, Tom stood his first watch. The next day, he went on his first patrol. Several days later, he first heard the two words that would become the hallmark of the rest of his tour: "Guns up." When a patrol suspected enemy activity, the machine guns would be brought to the head of the column to commence reconnaissance fire into the jungle.

Thomas J. Morrissey Jr.

CHAPTER 18

1976–1985, Massachusetts, Maine, and North Carolina

everal months later, Roz became pregnant. We were thrilled. She wanted to return to the Boston area to be closer to our families and hoped that such a move might have a positive impact on me. When we'd moved to New York, we had agreed that, unless one of us made it big, we would live there for five years. Neither of us had come close to big. I agreed with Roz that a change could be beneficial and shared her excitement about returning to the Boston area. My mood swings began to stabilize.

I found a new job with Johnson & Higgins (J&H), an international insurance brokerage. They agreed to relocate me to their Boston office after six months of training in the New York headquarters. While I knew nothing about the insurance business, J&H was a respected firm, the salary was good, and I liked the people I met during the interview process. My new boss said I had what it took to do well. Since I was determined to succeed, I took him at his word. Sarah was born on July 7, 1976. Six months later, the three of us moved into a small house in suburban Reading that was a short train ride away from my new office in Boston and close to our families, who now lived up the road in Andover.

The Vietnam War ended in 1975. As the last evacuation helicopter lifted off the roof of the American Embassy in Saigon on the chaotic afternoon of April 29, 1975, the ten-year conflict that had triggered the highest level of civil unrest in the United States since the Civil War, a century before, was over.

Americans couldn't forget the war fast enough. They also tried to forget our 2.7 million fellow Americans who had served in it. To many, we were the war. Our service was equated with the divisive American foreign policy that had sent us half a world away to fight and, in the case of 58,220 of us, die. Would they all now be forgotten? Would Tom Morrissey be forgotten? While huddled in my fighting hole, I may have been the only person to see Tom carrying the body of a wounded marine up to the LZ seconds before he was killed. How would his son ever know that his dad had died a hero? The remorse returned.

Since this was my third job in five years and I now had a young family to support, I kept my mouth shut and my head down. To stay focused, I tried to keep my Vietnam and Marine Corps past rolled up in a tight little ball deep inside of me. I didn't talk about it, and few people asked. Being a Vietnam veteran in liberal Massachusetts in 1977 was not exactly a badge of honor.

It was a satisfying time. Roz stopped working to take care of Sarah, we visited our parents on the weekends, and spent quiet nights at home during the week. I liked my new job, was stimulated by my coworkers, and got regular raises and promotions. This was how I thought life was meant to be. I was growing up. I could see no reason why it would ever change. We planned to have more children, dreamed of buying a larger home, and thought about getting a second car. I assumed my job would steadily provide for years to come.

Thwump.

The sound startled me.

In an earlier time, the unmistakable report of a faraway mortar shell rapidly exiting its steel tube would have instinctively caused me to seek the relative safety of a foxhole. On this evening, however, after a moment, my brain processed the sound as the routine ignition of our basement furnace. After several calming breaths, my heart rate lowered, and the hair on my arms relaxed. Since we were living in a new house, the furnace was a new and sudden sound. I soon adapted. But there would always be other sounds or sudden movements that would continue to set me off. For years after my return from Vietnam, I remained unconsciously alert and vigilant.

Ten years before, in the spring of 1968, as the leader of a 60-mm mortar squad, I had been on the giving end of the *thwump*. We used the mortar to launch parachute flares that would illuminate a nighttime encounter, white phosphorus rounds to mark potential targets, and high explosives to bomb enemy positions. That evening's *thwump* triggered me to recall the circumstances under which we had launched each of those rounds. On an average day, our team fired off ten rounds. Three might have been parachutes, one a white phosphorus, and the balance high explosives. We'd drop a round down the tube, hold our ears as it loudly thwumped back out, and wait for the evidence that it had reached its destination. A parachute flare would pop softly, high above, before it lit up the dark sky. A white phosphorus would ignite with a blinding light downrange. The high explosives would detonate, with a loud boom, several hundred yards away. On average, two of these rounds would not ignite. They were duds.

Having spent eight months on a 60-mm mortar team, I figured that I was responsible for about five hundred duds that lay unexploded somewhere in South Vietnam's Quang Tri Province. This armed ordnance, long ago covered by fresh vegetation, was waiting only to be triggered. At any moment, a local villager might come across one, pick it up, and fiddle with the nose detonator. I remain horrified that those lethal legacies of my year in Vietnam will live on for generations to come.

Our second daughter, Martha, was born on February 12, 1979. She was a joy. Like all new parents, we marveled at her matchless beauty, compared her looks and behavior to family members living and dead, and were astonished at how different she was from her older sister. All signs pointed to a positive future. Roz and I were happy in our marriage. The difficulties that had led us to counseling in New York seemed to be behind us. I felt financially and mentally secure and continued to do well at work.

In the spring of 1982, I was asked to open a new branch office in Portland, Maine. I was excited by the professional challenge and felt validated that my hard work had paid off. Roz was thrilled. She loved Maine, thought that it would be a great place to raise our children, and was excited that her family's summer cottage was an hour up the coast. We built a house in the town of Yarmouth. The day after the moving van pulled up to our Reading home, on August 8, 1982, our third daughter, Sylvia, was born.

My new assignment was challenging and, as my adrenaline again began to surge, I worked long hours to make the office a success. I hired a solid staff, produced new clients, and was happy with the results. Sarah entered the local elementary school. Martha joined her two years later. I could hardly imagine a better life. Roz managed our burgeoning family while reveling in all that was Maine. She loved the place. The schools were good, the neighbors friendly, and the pace was slower than Boston and New York.

Once a week, I drove ninety minutes south to visit my boss in Boston. Along the way, I'd pass through New Hampshire and mentally pause as I sped by the Dover exit. Did Norma and their son still live there? What about Tom's parents and siblings? But I never stopped. In the morning, I was focused on getting to Boston, and during my return in the evening, I'd be eager to get home. I did want to know about their lives after Tom's death, but not enough to again try to find them and make conversation about that awful day. It had now been fifteen years since his death. Young Tom would be nearing his seventeenth birthday. I wondered how much time would have to pass before I'd be able to muster the courage to face this family.

Soon after our move, open sores began to reappear on my arms, scalp, and face. I'd had a similar outbreak in the spring of 1968, when I was in Vietnam. I consulted a dermatologist, who diagnosed the ailment as discoid lupus, an autoimmune disease in which the body's immune system attacks its healthy cells. The treatment regimen was several dozen shots of cortisone directly into the lesions. I asked him if the affliction could have been caused by my wartime exposure to the widely used defoliant Agent Orange. He said that he knew little about Agent Orange and wasn't aware of any independent studies that had been conducted about its potential side effects.

I had seen news reports about Vietnam veterans who were coming down with a variety of cancers, including Hodgkin's disease and soft-tissue sarcoma, in numbers that far outweighed the national norm. That these afflictions may have been caused by our exposure to Agent Orange was emphatically denied by the government and the manufacturers. I wrote a letter to the VA in Augusta, enclosed the biopsy results, and asked if the sores might have been caused by my exposure to Agent Orange. Several months later, they wrote back and informed me that there was no compensable disability category for any Agent Orange–related ailments. They additionally wrote that unless I could prove that my sores had been diagnosed while I was in the Marine Corps, I had no case. The letter concluded with a reminder that veterans had a one-year time limit from the date of discharge to file physical disability claims. My time had long since passed.

Agent Orange, so called because of the orange stripes that were painted on its fifty-five-gallon storage drums, was a chemical defoliant that had been widely sprayed in Vietnam by the United States. The purpose was to eliminate all growing flora that could shield the enemy and to destroy the crops that fed them. The estimated nineteen million gallons of the toxin that were sprayed over South Vietnam between 1961 and 1971 defoliated about 15 percent of the country. It contained dioxin, which was later identified as a carcinogen by the Environmental Protection Agency (EPA).

My first exposure to Agent Orange came in 1968. During the month of January, we watched as the spray planes made their daily sorties back and forth across the DMZ. The white, viscous substance stuck to the leaves of everything that grew. It brushed off the jungle growth and onto our skin as we walked on patrol. It got into our drinking water. It blanketed the ground where we slept. There were traces of it everywhere we went during the winter and spring of 1968. My mother had sent me a camera in February. I took hundreds of pictures until late May when it surrendered to the elements. The contrast between the shots that I took when I first got the camera and those taken three months later was stunning. What had, in the winter, been a lush green jungle had morphed, by spring, into a desolate gray landscape with few signs of life in the trees, bushes, or vines.

After countless government studies and growing litigation by afflicted veterans, the manufacturers (Dow Chemical, Monsanto, and Diamond Shamrock) and the United States government finally acknowledged the inherent danger of Agent Orange to human beings. As a result, its usage in Vietnam was banned in 1971. By that time, hundreds of thousands of US servicemen had been in constant direct daily contact with it. The EPA did not ban the use of dioxin in the United States for another eight years. A group of Vietnam veterans filed the first Agent Orange disability claims with the VA in 1977. All were denied.

The most catastrophic legacy of the spraying was borne by the people of South Vietnam. Long after the Americans had gone home, remnants of the defoliant remained in their soil, crops, water, fish, and livestock. The government of Vietnam claimed that half a million children had been born with serious birth defects and that as many as two million people were suffering from cancers or other illnesses that they linked back to the defoliant. They further alleged that four hundred thousand people had been killed or maimed because of their exposure to Agent Orange. The United States government vigorously contested the four hundred thousand figure.

In the fall of 1985, Roz took our eight-year-old daughter Sarah to Washington, DC to visit her godmother for the weekend. They returned on Sunday evening filled with stories about their trip. During dinner, Sarah handed me a Marine Corps coffee mug that she'd purchased. It gave me a warm feeling to have my service acknowledged by her. My time in the Marine Corps had rarely been a topic of conversation around our house. She then produced a folded sheet of yellow-lined paper.

"Here, Dad," she said, extending her hand across the table, "I brought this for you, too." Her gaze was intent. She wasn't smiling. She was studying me to gauge my reaction.

I carefully unfolded the paper while looking back at her. Inside, the mostly blank sheet appeared to have lines of heavy pencil scribblings on it. She nodded toward the paper as a way of suggesting that I study it more carefully. I looked down again and, as my eyes adjusted, saw the name appear.

Sidney B. MacLeod Jr.

I'd known about the recently completed Vietnam Veterans Memorial but had given it little thought. My life had been moving only forward. I'd had no desire to delve back into my past, particularly my Marine Corps past. And yet there was Sid, jumping off the page with that broad smile, sharp blue eyes, and fifties-era blond crew cut. Sid had been my best friend through boot camp and my time in the States. We were separated when we arrived in Vietnam in the fall of 1967. He was killed near Khe Sanh the following May. I knew nothing at that time about the pencil-rubbings of names on the wall, which had become a popular way for families and friends to honor and remember their fallen. Something changed within me that evening. I knew then that I could *not* forget the dead. All 58,220 of their names had been chiseled into that black granite for eternity. No matter how hard I squeezed my eyes shut or tried to look the other way, they would always be there.

Had I the capacity to cry at that moment, I would have. I had not cried since the afternoon of June 5, 1968, when I saw Tom Morrissey's dead body. I'd fought the urge on several occasions since but had largely succeeded in burying the shock and the sadness that I had endured on that day. I did not cry after my father had died earlier that year or seven years later when my mother died. I just couldn't find the tears.

"Thank you, sweetie," I said as I got up from the table and walked around to give her a kiss. "This is amazing." I paused. "You have no idea."

As I sat back down, my mind floated off to a faraway place. Sid and I were having a beer and listening to the jukebox after work one day when we were stationed in Barstow, California. We each had a year left on our two-year enlistments. A Vietnam tour of duty was thirteen months. It looked increasingly like we wouldn't have to go.

"Well, Jackson," Sid began, raising his glass, "we may never get our names on that war memorial." We laughed. It was a standing—albeit morbid—joke among marines. The implication was that if we went to Vietnam, we'd never get out alive.

"Nobody's ever going to build a memorial to this war, Sid," I responded. "I mean, it's not like it's World War II or something. Besides, the government calls it 'a police action,' so it's not even really a war anyway. Plus, I don't think anybody cares."

As it turned out, the Vietnam War *was* big enough, a lot of people *did* care, and Sid's name *was* on it.

Coming back to the present, I looked across the table. "You know, Sarah, Sid and I used to laugh about this. We never thought anyone would ever build a monument to the Vietnam War."

I was overcome with sadness. I still missed Sid every day.

After four years in Maine, I was promoted to manage the J&H branch office in Charlotte, North Carolina. It was a big, visible job within the company. I was thrilled. I knew that it would be a challenge that would take my best effort to succeed. I remained concerned about my mercurial emotional state but knew that I was at my professional best when my adrenaline was surging during the early months of a new assignment. My family was uncertain about the move but supported me and were optimistic about the uncharted life that lay ahead. Our consolation was that our Maine cottage would remain a welcoming summer retreat.

Over Thanksgiving weekend in 1987, we packed up our new

blue Dodge minivan and headed south. It would be my first time in North Carolina since infantry training at Camp Lejeune, twenty years before. We were moving away from the place that we had all loved and where I had thrived. On the up-side, for the first time since returning from Vietnam, we were moving to an area that was friendly to veterans—especially Marine Corps veterans. Several large Marine Corps bases sat along the coast, and many marines, retired and on active duty, lived in North Carolina.

Once settled, we began to enjoy Charlotte. We remodeled our house and took weekend trips to the mountains and the coast. At work, I was enthusiastic, focused, and productive. I served on several local nonprofit boards, including the Economic Development Council of the Charlotte Chamber of Commerce. My superiors at J&H suggested that it could be helpful for business if Roz and I became members of a church and join a country club. After several months of investigating both, we joined neither. It was noticed.

One weekend, we drove down to Beaufort, South Carolina, to visit our friend, Ned Tupper. Ned was a Long Island native who had migrated south for college and stayed to attend law school. He was now the local judge and had a thriving law practice. Beaufort is a beautiful southern town. Our family loved it. Unlike Charlotte, it revered its history and historic architecture. It reminded us of New England.

Beaufort is also home to the Marine Corps Recruit Depot at

Parris Island. On Saturday morning, we paid a visit to the base, so I could show my family that piece of my history. There had been no prouder moment in my young life than the day that I graduated from Parris Island. To this day, I consider it to be among my greatest accomplishments.

As we toured the base, they gaped at the hundreds of green-clad boys marching in formation with rifles on their shoulders while drill instructors barked cadence in an indiscernible language. It was alien to them. It was creepy to me. Distant memories were triggered at every turn. I showed them the painted yellow footprints on the parade deck where incoming recruits, fresh off the bus, fell into formation for the first time while being besieged by a screaming drill instructor. I reflected on how innocent we all had been on the night that we arrived and how that moment had changed our lives forever. We drove past the mess hall where, on one steamy predawn August morning, I first met Sid MacLeod.

We were told every day, during those miserable months on Parris Island, that we were all going to Vietnam to kill "gooks and Commies" and that many of us would not make it back. While standing in formation, the drill instructors would tell us to look at the guy on our right, then look at the guy on our left. He'd then state that, within a year, one of them would be killed in combat. While engaged in this exercise, we never looked at ourselves. No one joined the Marine Corps to die for his country.

A month after we returned to Charlotte, open sores began

to reappear on my face and scalp. They were more severe than the earlier episodes. To combat the outbreak, I visited a dermatologist, who again began a weekly regimen of cortisone injections. After two months of treatment, they began to disappear.

I considered having the sores evaluated by the Veterans Administration, but having been denied years earlier, saw no point in again being told that they weren't war related or that even if they had been, the time limit for filing such a claim had long since expired.

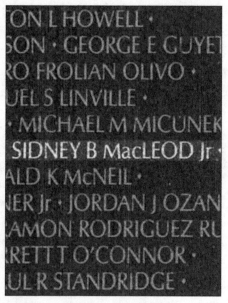

Sidney Macleod (Vietnam Veterans Memorial)

CHAPTER 19

1991–1993, Washington, DC

After sixteen rewarding years at J&H, I was offered a generous severance package, which I decided to take. It had not been a happy year for me, personally or professionally. My depression had returned and was having a negative impact on both my work performance and, more importantly, our marriage. At Roz's initiative, we again began weekly marriage counseling sessions which were beneficial, if not completely restorative.

After several months of searching, I settled for a position with a small insurance agency in Washington, DC. While it was not the major career change that I had been seeking, it would move us north and pay enough to cover our expenses. I began to sense that my once thriving professional career might be moving in the wrong direction. In early 1992, we purchased a home in suburban McLean, Virginia, and once again moved our family in the middle of a school year.

I wasn't sure if moving to McLean had been a coincidence or if I had been lured there by forces beyond my ken. Not only did the town share my name, but it was where Sid MacLeod had been born and raised. With the bittersweet memories of my old friend rekindled, I could feel Vietnam silently stealing back into my life.

One afternoon, in the summer of 1992, I walked from my downtown office to visit the Vietnam Veterans Memorial for the first time. Since the names of the dead are listed chronologically by date of death and I had a lot of names to find, I bought a book from a kiosk near the Lincoln Memorial that listed each victim alphabetically, with the hometown, branch of service, and date of death. I then walked over to the east entrance, found an empty bench, and began my visit by gazing at the flagpole and the larger-than-life bronze statue of three servicemen that overlooked the scene.

The Memorial was a powerful catalyst for changing the public's opinion of Vietnam veterans and our unique plight. Jan C. Scruggs, who had served with the US Army in Vietnam, was the driving force behind the creation of the Vietnam Veterans Memorial Fund that created the Wall. His goal was to create a lasting homage from the people of the United States to those who had served and died in the war. He wanted to separate the veterans' legacy of service from the widely renounced US policy in Vietnam and lay the groundwork required for national reconciliation.

Years later, Scruggs recounted a story about an early fundraising breakfast at the Georgetown home of Senator John

W. Warner (R-VA) and his then-wife Elizabeth Taylor, the legendary Hollywood actress. The Memorial Fund was running out of money, and political support for the project was waning. Warner was a navy and Marine Corps veteran of World War II and the Korean War, a former Secretary of the Navy, and a new member of the Senate Armed Services Committee. He was able to lure twenty-five potential donors, mostly defense contractors, to attend the breakfast, in exchange for healthy contributions that were intended to keep the Memorial Fund afloat. After breakfast, Warner and Scruggs spoke as the invited guests were folding their napkins. "Out of nowhere, Elizabeth Taylor appeared," Scruggs later recalled. "She walked down the stairs, and the person next to me actually dropped his cup of coffee." He went on to say that her only comment to the group was, "All right, you've contributed what you were asked, but not one of you is going to leave this room until you double it."

The money committed that morning spurred the congressional support required to appropriate two acres of land for the project on the National Mall near the Lincoln Memorial. Scruggs went on to raise $8.5 million from tens of thousands of individual donors. Other than the contribution of the land, the project received no government funding. The American Legion and the Veterans of Foreign Wars, the two VSOs that had, up until that time, doggedly opposed any congressional support to benefit Vietnam veterans, regarded any memorial to battlefield dead as a cause that was well within their mandate to support. Consequently, the two organizations provided the largest single contributions to the building of the wall, at a time when the success of the fledging project was still in doubt. Having joined the cause, they also gave their support, for the first time, to legislation that would address the needs of veterans suffering from the effects of their exposure to Agent Orange.

An open competition was organized to choose the architect who would design the actual memorial. Applicants were identified only by number, so that the committee would have no way of knowing the identity of any of the designers. The winner, by acclamation, was a plan presented by Maya Lin, an undergraduate architectural student from Yale University. Her black-granite V-shaped design was stunning. There had never been a war memorial like it. (*The Wall that Heals*—The Vietnam Veterans Memorial Fund)

Like the war itself, the memorial became divisive. While the Veterans Service Organizations, the press, and the public largely praised it, there were objections from members of Congress and influential business leaders. These centered on the architect's gender (female), youth (twenty-one years old), inexperience (this was her first design), and ethnicity (Chinese American), as much as the design. Then there was the design itself. Some initially likened it to a tombstone.

It was, however, apparent from the start that something exceptional was beginning to take place there. When the concrete base was being poured during construction, a young man came by with his late brother's Purple Heart and threw it into the slurry. The Memorial was dedicated on Veterans Day, November 13, 1982. The public response was immediate and overwhelming. From the day it opened, visitors brought pencils and pieces of paper to make rubbings of the names of loved ones. Some left trinkets including medals, dog tags, letters, photographs, and cans of beer at the base of the wall. A common promise made among Vietnam War combatants was, "If we ever get out of this, I'll buy you a beer when we get home." The National Parks Service and volunteers still gather these items every day and send them to a warehouse in Maryland, where they are catalogued and stored.

Within a short time, the Memorial became the most popular site in Washington DC, with more than one million visitors annually. One journalist called it "The most emotional ground in the nation's capital." Reflecting on the Wall years later, former President George H. W. Bush remarked that it "erased the unfair criticism that had been leveled at those who fought," and demonstrated that "serving your country in uniform is an honorable thing." Not long after the dedication, Senator John Warner commented, "I hope that every president, whoever he or she is, will go down there on their first day or two in office and take a silent look at that Wall by themselves and, if necessary, revisit it before they make the decision to send our young people abroad in harm's way."

Vietnam veterans loved the Wall, cherished its unique design, and were proud that it sat right in the middle of the National Mall, where everybody could see and visit it. Unlike the war itself and the veterans who had served in it, it had not been shunted off into some obscure corner of the capital. In 1984, two years after it was dedicated, the American Institute of Architects listed the Vietnam Veterans Memorial on its top-ten list of "America's Favorite Architecture," ahead of the Washington Monument, its iconic neighbor.

The Wall became a real symbol that the Vietnam War was over and that the healing had, at long last, begun. Jan Scruggs organized ceremonies every Veterans Day and Memorial Day. He also arranged special events throughout the year for veterans' groups, wives, mothers, children, and the siblings of the dead. Several years later, thanks to the dogged efforts of former army nurse Diane Carlson Evans, RN, The Vietnam Women's Memorial, which pays homage to the important role played by women during the Vietnam War, was commissioned and erected nearby.

I sat on the bench for an hour, checking off the names of the forty-seven boys whose memories I had come to rekindle. When I got up and descended into the sacred grounds, the first name I located was Sid's. *Sidney B MacLeod Jr (Panel 57E, line 28)*. His panel is near the end of the **V** that points toward the Washington Monument. It had been the rubbing of Sid's name that my daughter, Sarah, had made and presented to me during the Sunday dinner when we lived in Maine seven years earlier. Next, I located Tom. *Thomas J Morrissey Jr (Panel 60W, line 20)*. His panel is on the other side, near the end of the **V** that points toward the Lincoln Memorial.

The listing of the dead begins at the top of the innermost east-facing panel, continues out to the end, and is then continued from the end of the west-facing panels back at the center of the **V**. The panels memorializing the first and the last to die are, thereby, adjacent to each other.

The names of thirty-nine of the forty boys who were killed on Loon are inscribed on Panels 29E and 30E. They are mixed alphabetically among the 178 others who had been killed in Vietnam during those three days in June 1968. The fortieth Loon victim, Michael J. Kilderry Jr., was several panels further down the slope. We called him "Snowball," because of his bright-blond hair. He had been sitting on the lip of a foxhole next to me on the afternoon of June 5, 1968, when the enemy rocket and artillery barrage began. He had received, what appeared at the time, to be a minor shrapnel wound in his right lower back, below the bottom of his flak jacket. A hospital corpsman looked at the wound and had him medevacked to Delta Med in Dong Ha. He succumbed to his wound one month later, on July 6. He was, thereby, listed seven panels further down the slope. Five hundred thirty-seven other boys had been killed in Vietnam between the time Snowball was injured and the day he died.

As I ran my finger over the etched names, I wasn't sure what I was feeling. Touching each, I tried to recall the last conversation I had had with that person or a time when we had laughed at something stupid. I thought about being a part of so much violent death at such a young age. While staring into the reflective black granite, I had the odd sensation of looking at the name of a boy I'd known when we were both twenty years old and seeing my now-forty-five-year-old face staring back at me.

Veterans Day 1992 marked the tenth anniversary of the Memorial. To commemorate the occasion, volunteers read the names of the dead for three full days. I was scheduled to read at midnight on the second day. It was a chilly November night. I bundled up, arrived several hours early, checked in, got the names I was to read, and sat on the ground in front of the Loon panel, head bowed, trying to evoke some emotion.

There were two readers on the platform who took turns reciting the names. Their cadence was dirge-like—one after another after another. Every ten minutes, a new pair of voices would continue the drone. Close to midnight, with my head still bowed, I heard a familiar male voice start to read names. This was followed by an equally familiar female voice. I slowly looked up and there, before me, were President Bush and his wife, Barbara, taking their turns reading name after name. I watched them for several moments. There was no fuss and no obvious security. There were, perhaps, twenty-five people milling around at the late hour. When they finished, the two of them walked up the path toward Constitution Avenue.

I learned days later that the president, returning to the White House from a reception on Capitol Hill, had decided to visit the Wall to pay his respects. It had been only a few weeks since his election loss to Bill Clinton. Reporters said that he had been feeling "despondent." I liked Bush. He was one of us. He had served bravely as a young navy pilot during World War II. That gave him a lifetime pass, as far as I was concerned. By his presence, I could also see that he cared about Vietnam veterans. It was midnight on a cold November night, and there he was, taking turns with his wife, solemnly reading name after name of *our* dead. The president, a decorated World War II veteran, was acknowledging *my* service. It was a wonderfully satisfying feeling. When I read my list of names several hours later, I was standing taller. I was proud to be among these grand young sons who—many while by my side—had given so much.

In stark contrast, there was little positive feeling among Vietnam veterans for the incoming president, Bill Clinton, who would arrive in the White House two months later. Clinton had not served in the military, despite being in good health and out of college. Like many others of our generation, he had successfully employed every evasive maneuver that he could concoct to get his name off the Selective Service list of those eligible for the draft.

The following spring, President Clinton was invited to speak at the Memorial Day commemoration that was to be held at the Wall on Monday May 31, 1993. I took my ten-year-old daughter, Sylvia, with me to the ceremony. It was crowded, as expected. There was a roped-off VIP area in front of the stage at the center of the **V.** Behind the rope, several thousand people fanned out up the hill. Many of the attendees were Vietnam veterans. Sylvia and I worked our way up to the front near the dividing rope. I put her on my shoulders so she could see.

The ceremony began with a prayer, the Pledge of Allegiance, and the singing of the National Anthem. The distinguished guests, who included Chairman of the Joint Chiefs of Staff, General Colin Powell, were introduced. This was followed by the laying of wreaths at the base of the Wall by various veteran and community groups. Present on the stage that morning, in a wheelchair, was decorated Marine Corps veteran Lewis Burwell Puller Jr., who had suffered horrific wounds while serving in Vietnam. He wrote a book about his experience, *Fortunate Son*, for which he received the Pulitzer Prize. Puller's father, the legendary Lewis Burwell "Chesty" Puller Sr., was the most decorated marine in the history of the Corps. To this day, when the barracks lights are extinguished at the Marine Corps boot camps at Parris Island and San Diego, all recite the incantation, "Good night, Chesty, wherever you are."

When President Clinton was introduced, there was polite applause from the VIPs. Then, silently and without disruption, the Vietnam veterans behind the rope turned their backs to the stage and remained that way until he concluded his remarks. Sylvia asked why everyone was turned around. She knew something out of the ordinary was going on that day and never forgot the moment. The president himself was a draft dodger and the first American president in nearly fifty years who was not a military veteran.

After the ceremony, Sylvia and I wandered over to an area that was lined with tents and booths selling Vietnam War paraphernalia. It was set up every year to cater to Rolling Thunder, the motorcyclists who roared into Washington by the tens of thousands every Memorial Day weekend. I found a hat that had the emblem of the Third Marine Division and the words *Vietnam Veteran* on it. I bought it, proudly put it on, and spent the rest of the afternoon self-identified. It was my first-ever public display of that fact. It had been a remarkable weekend that began with the reading of the names. The late-night visit from President and Mrs. Bush had been uplifting. However, as Sylvia and I mingled among the thousands of visiting Vietnam veterans, I could feel myself bursting with pride. I was indeed one of them. I felt that I had, at last, come home from the war.

The Rolling Thunder motorcycle riders were among the most visible supporters of Vietnam veterans, POWs, and MIAs. They rolled into the capital every Memorial Day weekend from all over the country. On the day before Memorial Day, they staged across the Potomac River in the Pentagon parking lot before riding, en masse, across the Memorial Bridge, past the Lincoln Memorial, down Twenty-Third Street NW, and right on to Constitution Avenue to the Memorial, where they mustered for a silent ceremony. It is a spectacle that grew with every passing year. Originally, the riders were almost all Vietnam veterans, but it has since swelled to include several hundred thousand other veterans and supporters.

I have stood at the corner of Twenty-Third Street and Constitution Avenue to watch the parade of bikers several times over the years. It takes hours for all the riders, with American and military unit flags flying off the backs of their bikes, to pass. The roar is deafening—like rolling thunder. On those occasions, I have seen a solitary enlisted United States Marine in his formal blue-white Dress-A uniform, saluting the bikers while standing at stiff attention on the center median of Twenty-Third Street, near the corner where the bikes make the final turn. He'd stand that way for hours. Every so often, a spectator would dash out, dodge the oncoming bikes, and lift a bottle of water to his lips before running back into the crowd.

Semper fidelis, brother.

The Rolling Thunder veterans appeared, to most Americans, to be a ragtag band of unruly, unkempt, and seemingly unstable motorcycle riders who wore random pieces of their old military uniforms and had their unit patches and combat medals sewn or pinned to their hats and leather vests. This added to the national impression that Vietnam veterans were a bunch of combat-fatigued crazies.

And yet, while there appeared to be no outward signs of military discipline, most had served their country with distinction, took pride in being Americans, and revered the flag under which they had fought. Rolling Thunder grew into the nation's largest annual gathering in support of Vietnam veterans. The riders came together from all over the country to honor their fallen brothers at a time when few other Americans were inclined to do so.

Living in Washington, it was difficult to ignore the sacrifices made by those who had served throughout our nation's history. Stoic monuments stood at every turn. I was proud that the Vietnam Veterans Memorial was now among them. I felt validated. The Wall was playing a positive role in our recovery. Because of this, many vets felt a growing need to reconnect with their buddies, some of whom they hadn't seen since Vietnam.

Saluting Marine (Memorial Day Washington, DC)

CHAPTER 20

1967–1968, Dover

The months of Tom's absence were agonizing for Norma. She began working the second shift at Dover Shoe. Since her mother worked the day shift, Norma could drop the baby off when she left for work and pick him up when she came home.

She had little contact with the Morrisseys, although she and the baby did spend Christmas Day at the Lexington Street house. She and Tom's brother George also attended midnight mass at St. Mary's Church the night before. As winter turned to spring, however, Tom's siblings, including George, with whom she had developed a good relationship, followed their mother's lead and had increasingly little to do with her. If one of them spotted her on the street, he would walk to the other side to avoid any contact. In the past, Tom had been able to keep his family at bay. Now, months later, with Tom eight thousand miles away, it had become nearly impossible.

Cecile and Pete O'Brien were neighbors of Norma's mother and sisters, on the other half of the first floor of their Park Street apartment. While the families weren't particularly close, the O'Briens also had a young child, so there was a certain amount of neighborly back and forth when babysitting was needed. Cecile and Pete's day-to-day life was occasionally monitored by Norma's sister Debra whose paper-thin bedroom wall was shared by their living room.

In early February, Pete asked Norma for a short-term loan. He needed six hundred dollars to pay off some pressing debts and would pay her back in a few weeks. Norma had the money that she and Tom had been diligently putting aside in their savings account and, trusting soul that she was, made the loan. A month passed, then two months, without the loan being repaid. Pete largely ignored her more pressing overtures, saying that it would now be quite a while, if ever, before he could pay her back. Norma was panicked. The money composed most of the savings she and Tom had been putting aside and, furthermore, she hadn't told Tom. At her wit's end, she took Pete to small-claims court in April, where Pete testified that there never had been a loan. As there had been no paperwork, the case was thrown out.

Tom was doing what he could do to hold himself together and keep Norma strong from afar. His letters to her, such as one written on April 6, 1968, were newsy, honest, and direct about his combat life and filled with his loving feelings for her.

Hi Sweetheart

Forgive me for not writing for the past four days but we just got back from a blocking force. It was a two-day operation with 3/3 as the sweeping element. They said we got over a hundred gooks. I only got two that I know of. I saw them drop when I hit them. We had two killed and four wounded, none of them I knew too well.

I love you so much it hurts so bad. Honey, I want you to write me and tell me you're going to be mine forever, OK? Do you have any doubts about my love for you? I want to know the truth. You better not. If you do, I'm going to fix that as soon as I get home. I'm going to give you such comfort and devoted love, you aren't going to believe it.

By early May, with Tom having been gone for nearly nine months, their savings depleted, feeling the incessant stress of raising a one-year-old, and enduring the continued negative pressure from Lexington Street, Norma felt an overwhelming need to get away for a week or two to clear her head. She had a friend in Nashua who had been asking her to come visit, so she made the call. She wrote to Tom to tell him of her plans then asked her mother if she could watch the baby for a week or two. Her mother had recently been furloughed from the shoe factory, so had the time to provide continuous care.

Half a world away, Charlie Company was camped out just south of the Con Thien fire base along the Demilitarized Zone. Several of us noticed that Tom had not been himself that spring. He was troubled by something back home but wouldn't tell us what it was. We'd heard that he had spoken to Captain Negron and to the battalion chaplain to request emergency home leave. He said he'd be leaving in a day or two.

When Norma returned home the following week, all that had been positive and hopeful evaporated in a horrifying instant. Her mother had been called back to work so, to provide immediate childcare for the baby, she had taken him up to stay with Loraine.

Lorraine seized on the opportunity. Feeling that Norma had abandoned her grandson, she steeled her determination that she would never allow her to see her child again. She hired an attorney and drafted a public notice to go in the Dover newspaper, soliciting for information about the mother of a fourteen-month-old child named Thomas J. Morrissey III, as a first step to gaining legal guardianship. It ran for three days with no response. Norma was out of town, and her mother didn't read the paper. After the third day, Lorraine had achieved the legal basis needed for abandonment and immediately filed the court papers to obtain custody.

The petition, filed before the probate court for Strafford County, asked that temporary custody of Thomas J. Morrissey III be granted to Thomas and Lorraine Morrissey. It alleged that their daughter-in-law had deserted her child. They enlisted the help of Norma's neighbors, Cecile and Pete. Pete was still seething that Norma had initiated legal action for the $600 that he had borrowed months before. Still in financial straits, he was more than willing, for a price, to fabricate testimony against Norma. Debra, her ear pressed to her bedroom wall that was next to Cecile and Pete's apartment, became privy to the unfolding conspiracy. Still, on May 22, 1968, the probate court granted temporary custody and appointed Mr. and Mrs. Morrissey as guardians for their grandchild. Norma's father and mother were neither informed of the hearing nor permitted, after the fact, to add their testimony.

Thomas J. Morrissey Jr. was killed in action on June 5, 1968.

CHAPTER 21

1992, Washington, DC

On a gray November morning in 1992, sitting alone in my eleventh-floor office on Thirteenth Street, the memory of the Loon battle not only rose to the surface but demanded attention. I thought of the dead, their families, and my long-lost brothers in arms. For the first time in twenty-four years, I was eager to reestablish a connection with anyone who had been there. I thought if I could locate just one or two of them, we could begin the long walk back into the sunlight together. Then perhaps we could find others.

I recalled that Bill Negron had gone to Miami University in Ohio. On that November afternoon, I called the alumni office and was given his address in Scottsdale, Arizona. Several days later, uncertain that he would remember me, I wrote him a letter that began:

Dear Skipper,

There must be little in you that could recall me after twenty-five years back in The World, but your memory rekindles in me often in a most positive way …

I imagined that Bill and the others were attending reunions, remembering old times, and engaging in a form of camaraderie in which I'd had no interest. Now, for the first time, I wondered what had happened to them all. Would Captain Negron remember me? Did he remember Loon? Since my departure, he had likely fought in other battles that had left fresher scars.

I awaited Bill's reply with high anticipation that was tempered with low expectations. It arrived two weeks later.

> Dear Jack,
>
> There is still a part of my memory left that recalls you, not many of my troopers left Vietnam to go to Harvard.
>
> I've only been to the wall once; it was one of those snowy cold winter days that shuts D.C. down. My tears froze on my face. Yes, Charlie Company is well represented in black marble.

Bill Negron remembered me, and he remembered Loon.

Several days later, I was surprised to receive a letter from Bill's wife, Myrna.

> Dear Jack,
>
> The letter you wrote my husband, Bill Negron,

brought him to tears. He believes very strongly
that his kids from Vietnam may be suffering. He
feels responsible for every man that served with
him that didn't make it home.

It was reassuring to know that I had not been alone, and that
the nightmare was real. All those boys really *had* died. He later
told me that I had been the first Charlie Company veteran
with whom he'd had any contact. He too had been suffering
in silence. I realized that many of the others probably were as
well. That I was the first to find Bill said much about Vietnam
veterans and how alone we felt, if we felt anything at all.

Bill and I continued to correspond through letters, email, and
occasional phone calls. Three years later, I flew out to Phoenix
to see him. The last time I'd seen Bill was on the day I'd left
Charlie Company in July 1968. We recognized each other as
soon as I came out of the jetway. He was taller than I remembered but otherwise looked almost the same. We drove to a
bar in Scottsdale that was near his home, found a quiet booth
near the back, and spent the rest of the day drinking beer and
talking about our lives. He'd had a distinguished twenty-five-
year career in the Marine Corps that included a third tour of
duty in Vietnam. When he retired as a lieutenant colonel in
August 1981, he was the highest-ranking Marine Corps officer
of Puerto Rican descent.

The day flew by. We were joined by Myrna late that afternoon.
The three of us continued to share stories through dinner and
well into the evening. He told me that he'd been diagnosed

with PTSD and, at the slightest provocation, was capable of flying off the handle like a crazy man or sinking into deep bouts of depression. I shared my similar feelings and experiences and began to wonder for the first time if I too had been mentally impacted by the war.

After what had been a long and mentally exhausting day, Bill and Myrna drove me back to my hotel. As we were saying our goodbyes, Bill gently placed his hand on my shoulder and looked me in the eyes.

"Hey, Jack," he said, "I want you to get Charlie Company together again. A lot of those kids are still suffering out there. It's been almost thirty years. We're not going to be around forever. We need each other now more than we ever did."

Get Charlie Company together again? It had taken me twenty-five years just to find *him*. How was I going to locate two hundred more lost souls?

"Aye, aye, sir," I responded and executed a snappy salute.

While living in Charlotte, I had served on the Economic Development Committee of the Charlotte Chamber of Commerce. It was fun, and I'd learned a lot about marketing, regional business attraction, and community organizing. As a rapidly growing city in the "New South," Charlotte had wanted it all and wanted it right away. When I arrived in 1987, it was already on its way to becoming a national commercial banking center that would rival New York. While I was there, we attracted an expansion National Basketball Association franchise and a regional airline hub for USAir.

Because of my experience, I was asked in 1992 to organize and run a regional public/private business development partnership called the Greater Washington Initiative (GWI). My role on the board of the Charlotte Chamber during their go-go years was a plus. The partnership, created as a subsidiary of the Greater Washington Board of Trade, was the brainchild of its president, John Tydings, who became my boss. The GWI offered me a clean slate. It was an incredible opportunity. Operating funds for the first five years had already been raised. A board of directors, composed of the CEOs of the region's largest private employers and the top elected officials of each of the sixteen local jurisdictions, was in place. The sole goal that I had been given was to get the Greater Washington region onto the top ten of *Fortune Magazine*'s Best Cities for Business list. Charlotte had been a regular entry in recent years. Washington had never made it.

We got off to a good start. I authorized a study of our regional assets, created an international marketing plan, and got John Tydings and the board to buy into our strategy. We organized business-development trips to California, Canada, England, Germany, and Japan to raise awareness about the Washington region as a fertile location for science and technology business. These trips usually included members of the board. It was fun. It was exhilarating. After several early successes, I became a public figure, got good press, and was in demand as a region-boosting public speaker. At the close of our second full year of operation, we received notice that Greater Washington had made it, for the first time ever, onto *Fortune Magazine*'s Best Cities for Business list. We debuted at number two. I could not imagine a better job.

At the end of my fourth year at the Greater Washington Initiative, I had every reason to be happier and more ful-filled than I had ever been. Our efforts had contributed to a regional economy that, until recently, had only been known for its politicians and bureaucrats. New internet companies, like America Online (AOL), were cropping up throughout the area, particularly in Northern Virginia. I had hired and trained a talented staff, raised the funds needed to keep us going for another four years, and maintained the strong support of John Tydings and the board.

Then I began to slowly self-destruct. My attitude took on a negative edge. I became less patient with the board. I got into several public scuffles, one of which a furious John Tydings was able to keep out of the next day's *Washington Post* by engaging in some desperate late-night horse-trading with the reporter. I was also no longer being fully present for Roz and our three teenage daughters. Given my history, I knew that I was headed for a fall. I thought back to my evening in Phoenix with Bill Negron and began to seriously wonder if my time in Vietnam thirty years earlier could somehow be contributing to my errant behavior today. How would I find out? The VA? A private psychologist? I wasn't sure where to begin.

In the spring of 1998, I resigned from what had been a terrific job to start my own firm. I rationalized the move by thinking that I was uniquely equipped to provide marketing services to Washington's booming business community. Mostly, I wasn't thinking at all. It was a decision that exposed my growing hubris and marked the beginning of what was to become a ten-year downward spiral of personal and professional failures.

My new business, McLean Communications, got off to a slow start. While I was successful in landing several small clients, the investors were expecting more immediate returns. Rather than try to work out an equitable solution, I tried to dissolve the agreement. I thought that they had misrepresented the terms. They sued. Eight months later, to my enormous relief, the judge threw out the case, saying that it was baseless. It was a painfully distressing and financially exhausting period. I felt that I was approaching a point of no return.

Like most marriages, ours was not perfect. Roz knew this and had twice arranged for us to get marriage counseling. Had I been more forthright and honest about my feelings and my actions, our differences might have been resolved early on, but I wasn't. I'd had two extramarital affairs during our marriage. Each was filling some emotional void, or so I rationalized at the time. In the winter of 1999, I thought that I was ripe for another affair. Although there was no one else in my life, I could identify the signs. I didn't want to begin living inside of another lie. I finally understood the real hurt that I had caused Roz and our daughters.

In desperation, I found a therapist. At the beginning of our first session, she asked what I hoped to accomplish during our time together. I told her that I wanted to remove everything that was inside of me, spread it all out on the lawn in front of us, examine each item, and bring back in only that which could help me lead a saner life. Nothing and nobody, except for our three daughters, would get a free pass. Roz was worried about my emotional health. On several occasions that winter, she invited me out to the Arlington County Outdoor Nature Lab, where she worked as a teacher. She felt that time in the country might be therapeutic for me. Years later, she told me that she had feared leaving me home alone.

I met with the therapist three times a week. We began by talking about my marriage and children. We then talked about my father, mother, siblings, and early childhood. We talked about my business career and the success that I had had at the Greater Washington Initiative. One day, she asked me about Vietnam. I told her I didn't want to talk about Vietnam. I wanted to talk about what was going on with me *now*. Incredibly (in retrospect), she never brought up the subject again.

I had become emotionally disassociated from my family. To pull myself together, I told Roz about the prior affairs and said that, while I still loved her and wasn't *unhappy*, I just wasn't happy. That was the best that I could come up with. Rather than trying to work out our differences with outside help, I told her I wanted to end our marriage. It was a nightmarish period for the two of us and for our daughters. Sarah was about to graduate from college. Martha was living at home, taking a gap year between high school and college. Sylvia was a sophomore at Andover. We separated that June. Roz moved back to Maine, and I moved into an apartment in the District of Columbia.

The move offered me no relief. Once a week, I'd trudge up to my therapist's office, which was near the National Zoo. During one such session, she asked me to tell her about something good that had happened to me during the prior week.

After a thoughtful pause, I said, "Sunday mornings. Those are my times."

"What makes them special?" she asked.

"Well," I replied, "on Sunday mornings, I sleep in until about eight, throw on some clothes, and walk around the corner to the Omni Sheraton Hotel. I go to the newsstand, get a large cup of coffee, the *Washington Post*, the *New York Times*, and when they have it, the *Boston Globe*. Then I walk back home, take off my clothes, and climb back into bed."

"That sounds like a good start to any Sunday morning," she observed.

"Then I drink the coffee," I went on, "read the papers, and do the *Sunday Times* crossword. By then, it's usually about one o'clock. That's Sunday. The highlight of my week."

After a pause to determine that I had finished my thought, she said, "Well, Jack, next week, I suggest that you stay in bed until two or three o'clock."

At first, I thought she was being flippant, so I laughed. Then I realized that she was serious.

"Baby steps. Start with baby steps," she concluded.

I began to think that private therapy wasn't working for me. It had now been several months, and I needed more than baby steps. I needed some real strides. I was despondent and felt that I was becoming a danger to myself. On my way home from our weekly sessions, I'd walk over to the great ape house at the National Zoo to think about the session and watch the mountain gorillas. I could watch them for hours. That was the real highlight of my week.

During the long evenings and endless weekends in my new apartment, I'd sit with a glass of scotch in hand, listen to Leonard Cohen CDs, and stare across the room at an antique wooden side table that had belonged to my mother. I would imagine that there was a gun in the top drawer—a .45, like the one I'd carried in Vietnam. I thought about how easy it would be to walk across the room, open the drawer, slam an ammo clip into the handle, flip off the safety, put it in my mouth, and kill myself.

I hated guns and knew that I would never own one. Nevertheless, night after night, I stared at that drawer thinking about how effortless it would be if there *had* been a gun inside.

CHAPTER 22

1999–2000, Washington, DC

After locating Bill Negron seven years earlier, I'd been unsuccessful in finding anyone else from Charlie Company—not to say that I tried very hard. Bill would occasionally needle me about it, but mostly he let it lie. One day, however, I began to think of Dan Burton and wonder where he was and how he was doing. Dan had been my "foxhole buddy." During our year together in Vietnam, he'd had the ability to cheer me up under the worst of circumstances. I needed some cheering up. Very late one night, in the spring of 1999, I called his mother for the first time in thirty years.

"Do you have any idea what time it is?" she asked in a groggy voice.

After gathering herself, she peppered me for news of my life and health. Although I never did meet Dan's mom, a former marine herself, I had always felt a special bond with her because of those decades-spaced late-night heart-to-hearts.

After I hung up, I realized that I had forgotten to jot down Dan's number, so I called her back and woke her up again. I'd like to think that, had the tables been reversed, I would have been as gracious. She was a saint.

Dan and I connected that night.

The years dissolved when I heard his infectious laugh. I told him I was divorced. He told me he was divorced. I told him about my kids. He told me about his kids. He told me he was trying to qualify to become a golf pro. I told him about my visit with Bill Negron. He said he had not seen or spoken with any of our Charlie Company cohorts since his return in December 1968.

"Bill asked me to get Charlie Company together again," I said with a half laugh. "I'm not sure where to even start."

"Did you ever connect with Morrissey's widow and kid?" he asked. "Norma, right? Wasn't that her name?"

"Yes," I replied. "I mean, yes, her name was Norma. Their son was Tom III, but no, I never did make it up there. I wouldn't know where to start to find them now. Morrissey is a common name up in New England."

"What a hot shit he was," Dan said, almost to himself.

The conversation brought my mind back to our long-lost friend Tom. He and I had been friends. We shared a New England bond that gave us a touchstone within the geographic mixing bowl that was the Marine Corps. I never heard him grouse about an order, but he did have thin skin for what we called "typical Marine Corps chickenshit."

One memory made me laugh out loud. "Hey, Dano," I began, "remember that bullshit with the rakes when we were at the Washout?"

"Oh, yeah, brother. That was Tom at his best."

During a slow period near the Con Thien firebase along the DMZ, our platoon commander, Captain Renfro, ordered us to rake all the dirt around the compound, leaving nice little lines, then find stones to make paths between the bunkers. He even had the rakes sent up from the rear.

"I ain't rakin' no fucking dirt or making any silly-assed paths," Tom announced to anyone who could hear, while meticulously cleaning his weapons and sorting through freshly arrived cans of machine gun ammo. The rest of us laughed and silently wished that we could muster the same moxie. He was our quiet, albeit reluctant, leader. Tom only wanted to do his job well and get home safely.

And he could laugh and make the rest of us laugh. He'd spin story after story about some boneheaded thing that one of us had done on a patrol, ambush, or listening post. One of his favorite foils was George Hughes, his assistant gunner. George followed Tom around like a puppy. Tom also told stories about his ventures to York Beach and the strip clubs in Boston's notorious Combat Zone. We laughed with him, and we laughed at ourselves. He kept us loose. It was almost fun. Despite the circumstances, we were a hundred teenaged boys for whom humor, particularly at someone else's expense, could be funny. It was rarely mean-spirited or vindictive. We each hoped to be at the center of one of his stories. We liked his attention.

Tom rarely joked about the business end of being a marine. He was alert, his weapons were clean, and he was among the first to respond to any sign of enemy contact. At the call of "guns up" Tom, with his ammo-laden assistant gunner hustling behind, would scurry forward along the narrow flank of our patrol column like an engine headed to a fire. The rest of us would silently duck off the path to let them go by.

"Well, Brother Jack," Dan said, bringing me back to the present, "Now there's two of us. Sounds like we have a lot of lost marines to find if we're going to fulfill the Skipper's wish to get Charlie Company back together again. We'll just add Norma and the kid to the list."

The following year, in the fall of 2000, Dan and Bill Negron flew to Washington, DC, for a visit. Bill was able to locate several others who lived in the Washington area. After they arrived, we gathered at a local pub and spent a long evening together telling stories, remembering lost brothers, and trying to piece together the disparate fragments of our shared experience. There were many questions and few answers. We had each relived the experience, in solitude, for thirty-two years and developed our own alternate reality to get our minds around what was so painful to recall. When we finally staggered out of the bar, Dan, Bill, and I walked several blocks back up the slight hill to my apartment. We stopped several times to give Bill a chance to catch his breath. He said that he had been diagnosed with COPD, a lung disease likely related to his cigarette smoking. It was tough to see our once-mighty leader suffering.

The next day, Bill arranged for us to have a monument tour of Washington. Our guide was Don Price, a retired Marine Corps colonel Bill had served with during a posting to Washington. Don, an author and historian, showed us dozens of statues, old fortifications, a Civil War cemetery for Black soldiers, and other historical sites that few locals ever visited. Each stop had a compelling story tied to our nation's history. We were mesmerized. It was a memorable day in the company of a new friend and my dear long-lost brothers.

Dan and I drove Bill to the airport that afternoon to put him on a flight home to Phoenix. As he pulled his bag out of the trunk, he turned to us and said, "Go find the rest of Charlie Company and report back."

"Aye, aye, Skipper," we responded and saluted in unison.

Dan and I went back to my place, told stories, asked questions, and reveled in recounting our extraordinary weekend. Our assignment, which had seemed daunting to me years before when I first visited with Bill in Arizona, now seemed doable, thanks to the burgeoning internet.

Early Monday morning, Dan and I went to the Washington Navy Yard with the hope of finding direction for our project. The Navy Yard was the repository for the Marine Corps unit diaries from Vietnam. With the patient assistance of a resident researcher, we sat on the floor for hours, sifting through file after file from cabinet after cabinet. We located copies of most of the microfiche files of Charlie 1/4 for the years 1967 and 1968. Some were nearly indecipherable. Others were easily readable and provided valuable information.

Each unit diary included a roster, so we were able to reconstruct a partial list of long-forgotten names. It was a major step forward. Dan copied much of the information, took it with him when he returned to California later that day, and got busy on his computer.

One of the first people he found was Wayne Wood, who had been horrifically wounded on Loon. I'd last seen Woody in the amputee ward of the Oakland Naval Hospital on my way home from Vietnam. I called him immediately.

"Hey, Woody, it's Jack. Jack McLean from Charlie Company."

"Hi, Jack," he responded with his familiar slurred drawl. "How you been? Where you at?" It was like he was picking up on a conversation that had been interrupted minutes before.

"I'm okay," I said. "I'm living in Washington, DC. You still in Cedar Rapids?"

"Yeah," he responded. "Still here in Iowa, living down the street from where I grew up."

Woody had been wounded by the same round that had killed Tom. He'd lost one leg and the use of his other leg and an arm in the explosion. He had landed in front of me, about twenty yards from the blast zone. I was among the first to his side. He was screaming, which I took to be a good sign since, looking down at his bleeding, shredded body, he should have been dead. The corpsman quickly arrived and administered several doses of morphine. We wrapped him in a poncho and hauled him up to the LZ to be medevacked. Incredibly, he made it.

He was eighteen years old and had a girlfriend, Jan, who he was going to marry as soon as he got back home. When we were in-country, he talked about her endlessly. I'd asked him if Jan or any of his family had traveled out to Oakland to see him in the six weeks that he'd been there.

"No. Not yet," he replied. "I think they're planning on coming next month. Dad hasn't been able to get the time off from work yet, and Jan, well you know, she's still in school."

I'd thought of Woody a lot over the years—did his parents ever come to see him? Did Jan? He occupied a sad place in my heart but, until today, I had never tried to find him.

"Hey, you remember Jan?" he said. "Well, we got married when I got back, just like I said we would, and we got a few kids who are almost grown. I've been teaching at the local school."

My relief was palpable.

It was an exhilarating time. Thanks to the growth of the internet, hardly a week went by when I didn't receive an email with the subject line, "Another brother found." The new American century was off to a terrific start for the far-flung marines of Charlie Company.

Thurmond Moore, a former marine who had also served with the First Battalion, Fourth Marines in Vietnam, created our first battalion website. It provided helpful information to those of us who had served in the battalion, particularly the Vietnam veterans. The site included a posting board where visitors could make inquiries about marines they might be trying to find. After an inquiry was posted, Thurm would redirect it to those of us he thought might have the greatest chance of being able to act on it.

There had been little postwar unit cohesion since Vietnam. It took me twenty-five years to find Bill Negron. This was a common experience, and it contributed greatly to the isolation and alienation of many Vietnam veterans. It was impossible for someone who hadn't been there to credibly validate our experience. Consequently, most of us buried our wartime selves in holes and remained there for years. I have spoken to dozens of former comrades who still want nothing to do with me, Vietnam, or the United States Marine Corps. They served honorably, came home to an ungrateful nation, said "fuck it," got jobs, and tried to get on with their lives.

The internet changed that. While sitting at home, it was possible for a person with even limited computer skills to find a "missing" comrade-in-arms. As time went by, man by man, Charlie Company veterans began to return to the fold.

Thurm's early leads turned into a small movement. As we found new buddies, they'd come up with new names to look for. "Hey, you remember …?" "Let's see if we can find …." Postings would be made on our site and other Marine Corps sites. As Google rose to the fore, the searches became easier, and the successes came almost daily.

We were giddy with our success. Some of those we found had no memory of the carnage that had occurred on LZ Loon. Others remembered it in such vivid detail that I wondered how they had slept a night since. We began to have reunions. Vietnam veterans of all stripes were emerging from the holes within which we had buried our experiences. We were finally able to feel the catharsis that came with the understanding, acceptance, and acknowledgment, first among ourselves and then, over time, by the country.

It was a time of widespread validation. For the first time, we were allowed to be proud of our service and unafraid to show it.

Dan Burton, Bill Negron, & Jack McLean (at Memorial)

CHAPTER 23

May 2002, Knotts Island, North Carolina

The growing national acceptance of Vietnam veterans occasionally showed itself in unexpected ways. Many poseurs appeared who had not served in Vietnam but who wanted to catch an unpaid ride on our bus. According to the 2000 Federal Census, the number of Americans claiming to have served in-country Vietnam was a staggering 13,853,227. That meant that four out of five who claimed to be Vietnam veterans were not.

After years of ambivalence about our service, millions of Americans were now pretending to have served for their own self-aggrandizement. The group included several members of Congress, a Pulitzer Prize–winning historian, and the national commander of the American Legion. This does not include the thousands who did not see action and said they did, claimed to have medals that they had not earned, or promoted themselves to a rank higher than what they had earned. There are groups who pursue these people aggressively. Anyone can now go online to see if their neighbor who shows up in the town square every Veterans Day earned the Silver Star that he has pinned to his lapel. It made me furious. I used to spend hours—days—scanning websites anytime I suspected a poseur. I found several of them and was quick to call them out, whether they were in public service or just neighbors down the street.

In March 2001, Sylvia, now a senior at Andover, invited me to speak about my Vietnam War experience at a school seminar. I hesitantly accepted, since it would be the first time I had spoken publicly about my service. The cold March day was much like the one during my own senior year in 1966, when I had returned to campus and announced, to the stunned disbelief of all, that I had enlisted in the United States Marine Corps. On this day, fourteen of us—teachers, students, and I—sat in a large room with chairs pulled about in a circle. The kids were riveted as I spoke and asked insightful questions. What I saw before me for the next two hours was an emerging generation of curious and interested Americans who, unlike their parents, knew little about Vietnam. On that bleak early spring day, Sylvia launched me on the long-labored journey that led to my own recovery. It was a huge step.

After my return to Washington, I got a call from Dan, telling me that he'd located Terry Tillery. Terry and I had joined the second platoon of Charlie Company on the same day. He went on to become Bill Negron's radio operator during the Loon battle. I called him immediately. It was great to hear his voice.

Another brother found.

Terry had been raised in Canfield, Ohio, and now lived in Knotts Island, North Carolina, a small coastal community about thirty miles south of Virginia Beach. He worked as a construction manager, was married, and had three children. We spoke for an hour, recalling hilarious incidents and horrific encounters. Before the call ended, I told Terry about a recurring nightmare that had haunted me for years. I had never shared it with anyone. It had been a beautiful day, I told him. I came into this village and saw two smoking army trucks with dead bodies still inside. Beyond, there was a squad of disheveled marines who were heaping dead bodies onto an ever-growing pile of dead North Vietnamese soldiers.

"I mean, where do you put that, Till?" I said. "The pile must have been five feet high ..."

"That was no nightmare, Jackson," Terry said. "That was Cam Lo—during Tet. It really happened. I've got a magazine piece that was written about it somewhere. I'll send it to you. Those guys were from Delta Company. You were probably there the next day. You could have seen it."

That same surreal scene had been streaming on a closed loop inside of my brain for thirty-two years. As awful as that moment had been, I now knew that it hadn't been a nightmare. The nightmare had happened. It has rarely recurred.

I was struck by the depth and precision of Terry's memories. We had been together in the second platoon before I was

moved to 60-mm mortars in February. He had become the
Skipper's radio operator shortly before the Loon battle. Like
Dan, his transfer out of second platoon probably saved his
life. We spoke little of our current lives. They seemed tame
by comparison.

Several months after we spoke, in early May 2002, I made
the four-hour drive south to Knotts Island. We were thrilled
to be back in each other's lives after thirty-three years apart.
Like me, until recently, he had had no contact with any of our
Charlie Company brothers. I brought him up to date on Dan
Burton, Bill Negron, Wayne Wood, and several of the others
that we had now located. That night, he became determined
to find as many of our lost company as he could. Over the
next several years, he made good on his pledge. Terry was a
prolific Charlie Company veteran finder. He retrieved guys
from all sorts of holes where they had buried themselves over
the decades since the war.

Before we went to bed well after midnight, I asked Terry
where he had been posted after he left Vietnam. Having had
two years left in his enlistment, he told me that he had been
sent to the Marine Corps Sea School in Norfolk, Virginia,
to prepare him for service on board a naval vessel. When he
graduated, six weeks later, he said that he was assigned to be
the admiral's aide on the newly commissioned aircraft carrier USS *John F. Kennedy* (CVA-67). He would be one of fifty
marines serving on a ship that carried five thousand navy
personnel. If you had to be in the Marine Corps, it was good

duty. When the ship came out of dry dock, they deployed to the Mediterranean Sea—a common Cold War destination. Shortly before the ship's arrival at the port of Caen, France, they were informed that members of the Kennedy family were gathering for a reunion that would include a shipboard celebration.

On the day of the event, liberty was canceled, the ship was scrubbed, the planes were moved topside, and the lower hangar deck was decorated to look more like a high school gymnasium on prom night than the working aircraft storage and maintenance facility that it was. All hands were ordered to stand by to give tours to the family and answer their questions. The ship's band practiced while food and drink were prepared for the upcoming evening gala. At the appointed hour, Terry wore his full blue dress-A uniform and stood erectly next to the admiral with his back to the bulkhead. Scanning the dance floor, he noticed that Rose Kennedy, the iconic matron of the Kennedy clan, was walking in their direction. He could feel the admiral stand taller, so he stood taller. Mother of the late president and the slain senator, there was hardly a person in America who couldn't recognize Rose Kennedy on sight.

"Good evening, gentlemen," she said when she stood before them.

"Good evening, ma'am," the admiral responded.

Extending her left arm, she said, "May I have the pleasure of this dance?"

"Yes, ma'am," the admiral responded. "The pleasure will be all mine."

Caught momentarily off guard, Mrs. Kennedy stepped back slightly, shifted her gaze from the admiral to Terry and said, "Thank you, Admiral, but I was speaking to the sergeant."

And so it was that Sergeant Terry Tillery of Canfield, Ohio, on an evening aboard an aircraft carrier in Caen, France, danced with Rose Kennedy.

"Where did you learn to dance?" I asked incredulously.

"Never did," he responded, "but it didn't seem to matter to her."

"What did you talk about?" I continued.

"I don't much remember," he said with a slight smile, "just the usual shit, I guess."

The following day, we attended a large community picnic in Virginia Beach with Terry's wife, Nancy, and their three grown children. It was here that I was introduced to Jell-O shots— ice cube-size, vodka-laced Jell-O squares—that slid down like candy. We sat in lawn chairs, drank beer, sipped local moonshine, downed the colorful shots, and ate all manner of southern picnic fare that was continuously placed before us. Terry and I spent the afternoon locked in conversation about our time in Vietnam. Few parts of our shared experience went untouched. All the while, his daughter Kristen sat silently by our side, taking it all in. When the event began to break up and we were gathering our things, she pulled me aside.

"Jack, I just wanted to say thank you. That was the first time that I ever heard Dad mention a word about Vietnam. I mean, I know he was there and everything, but we could just never get him to talk about it."

I was amazed. Several months later, I recounted the experience to my three daughters. "Can you imagine?" I said. I felt like I'd talked about it a lot. For all those years, it was always close to the top of my mind.

"Dad," they responded, almost as one, "you never talked about it. Never."

I told Kristen that I had written long letters home nearly every week that I'd been in the Marine Corps, including Vietnam, and would happily share them with her. She leapt at the offer. When I got home the next day, I found the letters, had them copied, and sent them down to her. It occurred to me that, while I had written the letters, I had never read them—not even once. *Perhaps it was now time*, I thought to myself.

I didn't hear back from Kristen right away, so I mentioned this to Terry during a subsequent phone conversation. He told me that Kristen had indeed read the letters and passed them around to their entire family. A month later, I received a handwritten letter from Helen Joseph of Brooksville, Florida.

> We have never met, but I feel like I know you. I've read your letters and Terry and Nancy have told me so much about you. I am Terry's mom. When

Terry came home from Vietnam, he asked us not to ask him any questions. We didn't and I know it was a terrible experience, but your letters have been a big help to me in understanding.

That year was the worst of my life, as I'm sure it was for your parents. Reading your letters gave me some idea of what you two went through.

I was surprised. How, all these years later, could Terry's mom have had no idea about what he had done during his year in Vietnam? The next time I spoke with him, I mentioned the letter.

"Didn't you ever write home when you were in-country?" I asked.

"Yeah," he responded, "I wrote home every week."

"What did you say?" I continued.

"Mostly that the place sucked, and could she send me some clean socks. You know, shit like that." He concluded, "Didn't see any reason to get her worried."

Several months later, I received a large box in the mail with a Knotts Island postmark. Inside was a neatly folded denim jacket. When I held it up, I could see that there was a large American flag on the back, corporal's chevrons on the sleeves, and my service ribbons and marksmanship medals affixed above the left pocket. There was also an LZ Loon insignia, a patch honoring the 58,479 souls killed in Vietnam, and another that read, "U.S. Marines—Mess With the Best, Die Like the Rest." It was cool—the kind of jacket that I'd seen the Rolling Thunder motorcycle riders wear. I put it on. It fit perfectly and looked great. I noticed a piece of lined paper sticking out of the right-side pocket. I pulled it out and read the handwritten message.

Jackson

What do you think?

I made this up so you would have something to wear on Memorial Day, reunions, and show your grandchildren.

Semper Fi, Till

P.S. Figured a Yankee like you would never get one made for himself.

Terry Tillery & Jack McLean

CHAPTER 24

Summer 1968, Dover

The final approval for Tom Morrissey's emergency leave did not come in time. On June 5, 1968, a day after landing on LZ Loon, we endured a withering artillery barrage. Ten marines, including Tom, were killed, and a dozen more were injured in the attack. Tom had been killed while carrying an injured marine to a landing zone for medical evacuation. In addition to a Purple Heart, he was posthumously awarded a Bronze Star medal with a "**V**" to denote a single act of combat valor.

Norma has no recollection of where she was or who told her that Tom had died. She does recall that when she returned from Nashua, her son was gone and her husband was dead.

Tom's remains, along with the others that were extracted that day, were flown to the makeshift morgue across the tarmac from Delta Medical in Dong Ha. Two days later, on July 6, 1968, his casket arrived at Dover Air Force Base in Delaware, the nation's principal military mortuary. Several days after that, it arrived at the Portsmouth Naval Shipyard to be received by Norma and Tom's parents. It was one of the first times that Norma had seen them since her son had been taken from her weeks before.

After arriving at the base, Norma was escorted to a plain brick building, led down a long hallway, and ushered into a small conference room. There, sitting around a table awaiting her arrival, were representatives from the Marine Corps and air force, the local undertaker, and Thomas and Lorraine Morrissey. The instant that Norma entered the room, Morrissey leapt from his chair, grabbed her by the neck, and screamed, "You killed my son! You killed my son!" He was quickly pulled off and restrained.

Norma was devastated. She felt scared and alone in the presence of the intimidating gathering. As she composed herself, however, her own rage rose to the surface. With all the strength she could muster, she looked directly into Lorraine's eyes and said, "I want you to give me my son back."

Lorraine, quivering and furious, rose from her chair, walked over to Norma, and, while wildly stabbing an index finger at her, responded, "I'll give you your son back, when you give me my son back."

Court proceedings continued after Tom's death. The Morrisseys were given temporary custody of young Thomas until Norma was "settled and recovered." She was granted visitation rights, but her attempts to see her son were routinely rebuffed by Lorraine. Young, inexperienced, and without the money to hire a good lawyer, Norma was powerless. "That's what I had to deal with," she later told me. "I was railroaded. I had no way to stand up to these deceitful, underhanded people, and they knew it."

Several months later, the Morrisseys moved out of state and left no forwarding address. Norma sent letters and presents to her son at the Dover address, but they were returned unopened. She spent the next eleven years searching for him. By the time she found out where they lived, he was thirteen years old.

"The Morrisseys' behavior put them in contempt of court," she later said, "and I had a good case against them. But I did not want to disrupt my child at that still-tender age. I resigned myself to the fact that I would probably never see him again."

Thomas Morrissey Jr funeral

CHAPTER 25

Georgetown

A week after returning from Knotts Island in May 2002, I met Karen Nicholson, a successful real estate agent in Georgetown. Karen was a red-haired beauty who returned long-absent joy to my life. We began an intense courtship that concluded with our marriage three months later. I still didn't have a job and was running out of money. She was a recovering alcoholic who hadn't had a drink in twenty-two years. Neither of these was of concern to either of us at the time. They probably should have been.

One afternoon, while consolidating our lives, we spent an afternoon at my apartment, deciding what should stay and what would go. After several hours, with garbage bags stacked high by the front door, Karen found the shoebox with my Vietnam letters.

"What are these?" she asked as she carried the box into the living room.

"Those are my letters," I replied. "The letters I wrote home when I was in Vietnam."

"What do you want to do with them?" she asked dispassionately, while holding them precariously close to the trash bag.

"Let's save them," I replied. "My mother always thought that I should use them to write a book about Vietnam."

"So … why don't you?" she asked.

It was a good question for which I had no simple answer. I was out of work and, for the time being, anyway, had time on my hands. I remembered the impact that the letters had had on the Tillery family. Perhaps they would be of interest to others out there. Later that day, I began to read them for the first time.

The following evening, I randomly pulled out a letter to my mother that I had written in April 1967. I had been stationed in Barstow, California, at the time, making barely one hundred dollars a month while working nights in a supply warehouse. It rekindled the memory of a weekend trip that Sid MacLeod and I had taken to Las Vegas that spring. While sitting at a twenty-five-cent poker machine, a waitress continually provided us with free drinks and cigarettes. Late that night, we cashed in our modest gains, got something to eat, and crashed at a cheap motel. The following morning, we boarded the bus for the two-hour trip back to Barstow. Though nursing severe hangovers, we had amassed enough cigarettes to last us until payday.

When I read Sid's name that evening, I became transfixed by events that I had long since tried to forget. It struck me that Sid was then and forever would be twenty years old. He would never go to divinity school—something he had decided to do only weeks before he was killed. He would never get married, raise a family, bury his parents, visit the Wall, or see the twenty-first century arrive.

He was dead. I mean, he was *really* dead. Then I thought of Tom Morrissey. He was really dead too. I wondered again, as I often did, about Norma and their son. Where were they? *How* were they? I was afraid to conjure up other names but couldn't stop myself. Joe Klein, Michael Kilderry, Woody Carbaugh, Felix Flores … and they kept coming … thirty, forty, name after name. My stomach clenched. My throat began to close. Breathing became difficult. And then, after decades of emotional suppression, I began to cry. And I continued to cry. Karen rushed in and found me lying on the floor in a fetal position. I was inconsolable. She stayed and softly rubbed my back while trying to engage me, but to no avail. All the emotions that had been so deeply buried oozed to the surface. I'd stop crying for a few seconds and then start up again. I started to laugh because I thought it was funny that I couldn't stop crying. Then I would continue to cry.

I spent the rest of the evening curled up on the floor while releasing a tsunami of grief from which I could find no shelter. The *me* of my youthful expectations that had been lost decades before on a faraway hilltop was reasserting itself. I was becoming free.

I cried for my parents, whom I had lost years before, and I cried for myself. I realized now how fortunate I was to have not only survived the carnage, but to have raised three daughters, earned a good living, laughed, gazed at lingering summer sunsets, and lived the life that those dear lost boys never could.

The next day, I began to transcribe the letters. As I wrote, I added notes and memories to help fill in the blanks. I had known that something was not right with me—the failed marriage, the unsuccessful jobs, the anger issues—so writing became the therapy that allowed me to probe the feelings that I had been unable to explore with my therapists. What began as a *what-did-Daddy-do-in-the-war* project for my three daughters became a journey of self-enlightenment and post-traumatic growth. Still unemployed with time on my hands, I began a daily immersion into my Vietnam experience. As I wrote, I began to see myself in new ways. I realized that for years I had been the cause of many of my own problems. I wondered if and how I could atone for my past behavior. While I felt understood, supported, and loved by my daughters, I needed to redress the damage that I had inflicted on them and their mother.

Meanwhile, the search for our lost brothers continued. Having Woody, Dan, Terry, and the Skipper back in my life motivated me to find more. There had to be other guys out there who needed help. One morning, after two years of looking, I finally got a Google hit on "Doc" Mac Mecham. Mac had been our navy hospital corpsman. On June 5, 1968, his thumb had been severed by a piece of shrapnel on Loon—shrapnel from the same rocket that had wounded Woody and killed Tom Morrissey. Mac and Woody had been medevacked together. My search revealed that a Mac R. Mecham had recently received a promotion to branch manager of a California medical equipment company. I stared at the screen in disbelief. How many people could there be who had that name, lived in California, and were in the medical industry? I called the listed number, gave my name to the receptionist, and waited.

Although the Marine Corps is part of the navy, my interaction with that service branch had been limited to "Doc" Mac and the hospital corpsmen who were assigned to each of our combat platoons. They were a special breed. Trained to provide immediate medical assistance on the battlefield, corpsmen were by our sides for every enemy encounter. They were the first to be thrust into the line of fire to help an injured marine and were, consequently, prized targets for enemy snipers. Most exhibited the same selfless bravery under fire that had been the hallmark of the Marine Corps for nearly two centuries. During the Vietnam War, four corpsmen received the Congressional Medal of Honor. An additional fifty received the Navy Cross, the navy's highest award for valor in combat. United States Navy hospital corpsmen are, rightfully, revered by all combat marines.

After a minute on hold, the music stopped, the phone clicked, and I heard the sweet sound of a voice that snapped me back nearly forty years. "Is this the same Jack McLean who used to burn shitters in Vietnam?"

"Doc," I sputtered, "is that really you?"

"Yeah, well, who else would it be?" he said, softly laughing. "How the hell did you ever find me, but more importantly, how the hell are you, brother?"

"Doc" Mac. Another brother found.

We talked about our lives and our families. He told me that he lived in Sacramento, was married, and had two grown children. I filled him in on Dan, Woody, Terry, and the Skipper. In closing, we agreed that our first order of business would be to figure out a way for us all to get together.

*Terry Tillery, Bill Negron, Dan Burton, Mac Mecham,
& Jack McLean (in San Francisco)*

CHAPTER 26

March 2003, Knotts Island

The following year, in March 2003, Terry invited some of the buddies we'd found down to Knotts Island to attend the Hunter's Feast, an annual celebration of the region's history as a haven for duck hunters. We stayed in an old lodge near Terry's house. Most of us hadn't seen each other since Vietnam. Terry began the weekend by giving each new arrival his own custom-made denim jacket.

Being alone together, we felt free to talk about the weight that many of us had been carrying since Vietnam. It was the first time some of them had spoken about the experience to anyone. Some bore the obvious physical wounds of combat, such as missing limbs and bullet and shrapnel scars. Others were hosts to the festering cancers that may have had their origin in the contaminated water that we drank while training in Camp LeJeune, or the Agent Orange that was sprayed on us in Vietnam. Most had been divorced, cycled through multiple jobs, arrested for felonies, or imprisoned. I was but one among them. We spent the next three days eating, drinking, laughing, telling stories, nursing hangovers, crying, smoking pot, and sleeping. Throughout the weekend, Terry quietly pulled each of us aside to talk about filing a disability claim. He was adamant. I remember well the first time he broached the subject with me.

"Jack, you ever talk to the VA about getting a disability for your service?" he asked.

"Yeah," I replied. "I did a whole bunch of years ago when I was having skin problems that I thought might be related to Agent Orange. They didn't want to hear about it—just slammed the door in my face. But what do you mean by disability?" I asked. "I'm not disabled."

"You served with a Marine Corps infantry company in Vietnam at the height of the fighting," he said, "right?" I nodded. "In one three-day period," he continued, "forty of your buddies were killed and another one hundred were wounded, including you. Right?" He didn't wait for my response. "And you never think about that?" He paused. "You don't think Vietnam fucked you up at all?"

"Well, yeah," I said. "Of course, I think about it …"

"I mean, you've had what …" he continued, "three or four jobs in the last four years and got divorced?" I nodded. "And you think you're okay? Think about it, brother. You're as fucked as the rest of us, Jack." Terry paused and stared into my eyes.

"File a claim, Jack. All they can do is turn you down, but they won't." He went on to tell me how to go about it. "You go to a VSO like the VFW or the VVA, give them your DD-214, and tell them your story. They fill out the forms, file with the VA, and do the follow-up. That's it. Oh, and one more thing," he went on, "whether you win or lose, appeal the decision. Get it? Appeal, appeal, appeal."

"Why would I appeal if I won?" I asked.

"Because they'll low-ball you the first time," he answered. "Always appeal—no matter what, because they will always try to fuck you."

I was thrilled to see Buck Willingham at the gathering that weekend. A former Charlie Company machine gunner, I'd last seen Buck at a battalion reunion two years earlier. After a welcoming hug, he stuck out his hand and gave me a folded piece of paper.

"Here," he said, "take this before I forget. Janie asked me to give it to you." Janie is Buck's wife. "I told her you were doing some writing about our time in Nam." With that, he handed me a long, handwritten note. I started to open it but decided to wait until I got home, so I put it in my pocket.

Buck and I had served together for eight months. He had been a fire team leader in the second platoon when I arrived in-country. Several months later, he became the company radio operator. Born and raised in Maysville, Oklahoma, Buck was short, thin as a rail, and spoke with a south/central Oklahoma twang that could be a challenge to comprehend. He seemed an odd choice for the job of radio operator, both because of his accent and the fact that the radio was nearly as big as he was. Despite that, he was an outstanding marine—calm, rarely rattled—and well-liked by all of us.

Janie, the daughter of a sharecropper from outside of town, had been his high school sweetheart. They got married in the summer of 1968 after his return from Vietnam. Since Buck had two years left on his enlistment, they spent the early months of their marriage living at Camp Pendleton while he attended Sea School in preparation for his next assignment which, like Terry Tillery, would be serving on a naval vessel.

When his ship, the nuclear-powered guided-missile cruiser USS *Long Beach* (CGN-9), came out of dry dock, Janie returned to Maysville, and Buck spent the next year cruising in the Gulf of Tonkin within sight of the South Vietnam coast. He had been told that their mission was to pick up downed navy aircraft-carrier pilots who might ditch in the gulf on their way back from inland bombing sorties. He'd suspected, however, that their real mission might have had more to do with the nuclear warheads that were carefully stowed below.

When his tour of duty was over, Buck returned to Janie in Maysville, where they still live in a house across the alley from the one in which he was raised. Through a friend, he got a job working in the oilfields, which he continued to do until he retired several years ago.

That Sunday evening, after I got home, I sat down, poured myself a glass of scotch, and read the handwritten note from Janie that he'd given me.

"I didn't have a clue," she began and continued:

> Through the years with our ups and downs it appeared as though Buck was trying to run away from something. He hardly spoke of Vietnam, just little bits and pieces. It was like he wanted to be proud of being a Marine but wasn't sure if he should. I was always patriotic and loved my Marine, but that didn't seem to matter. After years of living with his crazy actions, I just wanted to yell and say, "You survived! Why can't you just be happy?" Something seemed to be boiling inside.

> (Fast forward 35 years)

> Now that he has finally connected with his brothers there is peace. He now knows that his service was worthwhile, and he is proud of being a Marine. It is so cool that you guys have this bond, love, and respect for each other. Seeing you Brothers together and hearing your stories is something that touches my heart and has brought me to an understanding.

> Now, at last, I think I get it!

Buck Willingham & Terry Tillery

CHAPTER 27

November 2003, Washington, DC

Positive changes were starting to take place in the emotional and physical care of Vietnam veterans. On March 15, 1989, the Veterans Administration was renamed the Department of Veterans Affairs and elevated to a Cabinet-level department. During the following decade, thanks to renewed congressional awareness and an influx of federal funding, far-reaching structural improvements were made that led the organization to dramatically change for the better. In now providing much-needed help to *all* veterans, the VA is far ahead of where it was during the 1960s, 1970s, and 1980s, when the bulk of Vietnam veterans were routinely denied healthcare and disability benefits.

These improvements did not take place in a vacuum. It took years of persistent lobbying, most notably by Bobby Muller, a paralyzed US Marine Corps veteran from Great Neck, New York. Seeing that established veterans' groups had failed to address the issues of concern to Vietnam veterans, he founded the Vietnam Veterans of America (VVA) in 1978 to unite and leverage the previously disparate and disorganized Vietnam veterans into a powerful political force. The VVA received a Congressional Charter in 1986. This meant that they, like other accredited veterans service organizations, could represent veterans filing disability claims before the VA. It became the largest and most influential advocate for identifying and establishing remedies for Vietnam veterans' unique issues—readjustment counseling, PTSD, and the effects of Agent Orange exposure.

On November 3, 2003, after years of fruitless talk therapy with civilian psychologists and continuing concern about my mental health, I finally decided to see if the VA could help me. Terry Tillery had urged me to file a disability claim for PTSD, but before I did, I wanted to speak with someone who could tell me if I really did have an actual combat disability or if I was just fucked up. Armed with my passport and DD-214 discharge papers, I drove across town to the Washington, DC VA Medical Center on Irving Street. Along the way, I recalled my last (and only) visit to the VA shortly after my return from Vietnam, when I went to the Boston office to apply for the GI Bill benefits that would help me pay for college.

The registration office was on the ground floor. I gave the clerk my DD-214. She gave me a clipboard with a questionnaire attached and directed me to one of several plastic chairs outside of her office. After sitting down, I gazed up at the wall across from me and saw two photographic portraits. The one on the left was of Anthony Principi, secretary of the Department of Veterans Affairs. The one on the right was of George W. Bush, the forty-third president of the United States. I thought back to the VA office in Boston when I was applying for the G.I. Bill. Then, it had been a portrait of Lyndon Baynes Johnson that had caught my eye. The country had had seven presidents since then.

Life is funny, I thought to myself. President Bush and I had spent three years together as students at Andover. Now, four decades later, he was blankly smiling down at me as I was completing the questionnaire that might well save my life.

Halfway down the first page of the questionnaire, there was a box to check if I had ever had suicidal feelings. While I had experienced such feelings, I had never tried to kill myself. Still, the question asked about suicidal *feelings*, so I checked the *yes* box and moved down to the next item. Paperwork completed, I returned the clipboard to the clerk. Ten minutes later, she called me into her office, confirmed several items, took my picture with a camera affixed to her desk, and produced my official VA identification card. In closing, she said, "They want to see you in room 423 immediately, Mr. McLean. The elevators are out the door to your left."

I thanked her, put the card in my wallet, and walked to the elevators. When I got to the waiting area for room 423, I was told to have a seat. Before I could, however, my name was called.

"Mr. McLean?" I turned and saw a man in a white lab coat standing by the door. I nodded in acknowledgment. "Please come with me," he said. He was all business.

I followed him down the hall and into a small conference room, which was occupied by three other white-jacketed people. Two were psychiatrists. The other was a psychologist. From that moment on, I was treated with all the respect and urgency of a live hand grenade. In retrospect, I probably was. Forty-five minutes later, after answering questions about the state of my life and my emotional health, I was admitted to the hospital for a night of observation. The next morning, having determined that I was not an immediate threat to myself or anyone else, I was discharged and ordered to enter the VA's nine-month PTSD protocol.

There were eight other Vietnam veterans in my PTSD group. We met at the VA Medical Center once a week with a staff clinical social worker. He guided us through session after session of education and treatment. Attendance was mandatory. We were all relieved to be in the hands of capable professionals and began to develop the confidence that we might get better. I looked forward to each session, liked the other vets, and enjoyed doing the work with them. We acknowledged that we were all "nuts" and occasionally argued playfully about who was the craziest. As our stories unfolded over the following weeks, it became obvious that there would be no clear winner.

During the program, Otis, one of our group, died of a heart attack. An army veteran, Otis drove a postal truck from suburban Maryland to Northern Virginia every day. He spoke with a barely discernible lisp and regaled us with his daily driving adventures on the Washington Beltway. While he did not intend to be humorous, his stories often left me in stitches. When I'd laugh, he'd laugh, and the others would join in. Otis was a wonderful man. I never would have met him had I not been diagnosed with PTSD.

Byron, another member of our group, was homeless. Sometimes I'd drop him off at a downtown park so he could get one of the sandwiches that volunteers passed out at lunchtime. Every so often, I'd drive by in the late afternoon and give him a ride back to the homeless shelter on New York Avenue or to his sister's house in northeast Washington. One day, Byron didn't show up for our weekly session. We heard that he wasn't keeping his VA medical appointments either. We never saw him again. Like so many others, he was now lost out there somewhere.

In early April 2004, we arrived at our weekly session to find a stranger in our midst. A VA psychiatrist had come to take stock of our collective state of mind. He told us that, given recent events, the VA was concerned about our group. During the previous week, in the city of Fallujah, four US military contractors had been killed and mutilated, and five US soldiers had been killed by a roadside bomb. They feared that some of us might suffer setbacks. There was growing concern that the Iraq War, initiated by President George W. Bush a year earlier, might be escalating into a Vietnam-like quagmire.

I was distressed that we had once again invaded a foreign country without apparent cause. Had the United States learned nothing from *our* Vietnam experience? It had taken me thirty-three years to finally walk into the VA Medical Center to get the help that I needed. That meant that three decades from now, a combat veteran from *this* war might wander into a VA Medical Center in search of the help that *he or she* needed. Would the VA still be adequately funded by Congress? Would there still be a VA?

In addition to our group therapy, I met with a VA psychiatrist once a week to discuss my recovery and check the efficacy of the medications he'd prescribed. In his presence, I felt normal, understood, and at peace with myself. I looked forward to our appointments. Unlike my experience with private therapists, we talked about Vietnam at every session. There was a bottomless well with which to work.

Prompted by several members of the VA Medical Center staff and the continued urging of Terry Tillery, I applied to the Veterans Benefit Administration for a government disability for my now-diagnosed PTSD. I enlisted the assistance of the VVA, who had the authority to present the case on my behalf. While the VA reviewed my medical and psychological records, they had me examined by an outside psychiatrist, who conducted what is called a Compensation and Pension (C&P) examination. The whole process took several months.

In February 2005, I was granted a 30 percent disability for combat-induced PTSD. They had determined that, while I was having some trouble functioning both socially and at work, I was able to take care of myself and speak normally. My symptoms included depression, anxiety, chronic difficulty sleeping, mild memory loss, suspiciousness, and occasional panic attacks. It wasn't a lot of money—several hundred tax-free dollars a month—but it was validating to have my service and the resulting affliction recognized.

After reading the decision, I called Terry Tillery to tell him the good news and thank him for his encouragement and support.

"You file the appeal yet?" he asked.

VA PTSD Group class trip to the Vietnam Veterans Memorial

CHAPTER 28

August 2007, Washington, DC and Knotts Island

Meanwhile, I kept writing. I was pleased with how the book was progressing and began to make inquiries about getting it published. I thought that sharing my experience with a wider audience might help other veterans who were still trying to find their way.

Karen and I celebrated our fifth wedding anniversary in August 2007. We'd bought and renovated a house in Georgetown, had two little dogs, supportive friends and family, and spent quiet winter evenings reading by the fire. We were happy. There were underlying tensions, however. I had been hired and fired from two jobs during that time, and she was feeling the stress of a down-turning real estate market. We thought that we might have to sell the house to keep our heads above water. She was also increasingly frustrated with my PTSD recovery and, because of the time spent writing my book, everything that had anything to do with Vietnam.

I tried to remain positive. I was confident that my nearly completed manuscript would find a publisher, excited about my future as a writer, and pleased with the progress that I had been making with the VA. Karen wasn't so sure.

In August, we drove up to Maine for the marriage of my daughter Sylvia. It was a happy family time and a nice break for us. On the way back to Georgetown, we spent two relaxing days at a small inn in Cape May, New Jersey. When we got home, there was a fat FedEx envelope stuffed inside our front storm door. I was thrilled. After eight months of back and forth, I knew that the envelope contained the final suggestions from my editor on *Loon*.

After voicing my excitement, Karen flatly asked, "So, are you going to go down to the beach house to finish the book?"

It was a fair question. On several occasions over the past year when I'd received such edits, I'd gone down to an empty beach house on the Outer Banks that Terry and Nancy Tillery had bought the year before. It was a quiet place in a lovely spot that was far from the distractions of Georgetown.

"I'm not sure." I replied. "We've had such a nice week. I hate to leave." It wasn't exactly a lie, but it wasn't the whole truth either. We had been having a nice time. We were feeling closer than we'd been in months. But I did want to leave. I couldn't wait to get to work on the contents of the envelope, which was still laying at our feet.

"Go," she said with a soft smile. "You'll be happier if you do. It will only be a couple of days. I think we can endure that."

"Okay," I said, as I picked up the envelope and took our bags into the house. A half hour later, I emerged with an overnight bag and my pencils, pens, laptop, yellow pads, and the envelope, and put them in the still-warm car. I made a second trip for the printer and a package of paper. After a kiss for Karen, I put the car in gear and began the five-hour journey to the Outer Banks.

Three days later, the book was finished. It was an enormous relief, and I was thrilled. I had two copies printed off. One I sent to my agent in New York. The other I signed and hand delivered to Nancy and Terry. As I was leaving their house, I mentioned that Karen and I had been having problems and that I wasn't sure what I'd be walking into when I returned.

Terry tried to put me at ease. "If you run into a hot LZ up there, Corporal, there's always the Knotts Island garage." The three of us laughed at the prospect. Terry and Nancy had recently built a garage with a small apartment on a parcel of land they'd purchased on Knotts Island.

Four hours later, I arrived back in Georgetown, parked the car, and walked up the steps to our front door. Karen was waiting.

"I've had enough," she announced shortly after I walked in. I was caught completely off guard. "This isn't what I signed up for. You don't have a job, you don't have a book, and now I find out that you're crazy. And oh, I'm not going to sell my house."

I wasn't sure what to say. "Well, it is actually *our* house," I stammered. "And the book is finished. I sent it to my agent this morning. She's confident that she will find a publisher. It's all good news."

"The book?" she responded. Her voice was rising. "The *book*! I don't care if I ever hear the word Vietnam again."

I tried to stay calm. I had no idea where this rage was coming from. "Don't quit before the miracle happens," I finally said. It was an affirmation from Alcoholics Anonymous that she had recited to me at times when I became discouraged.

"There's not going to be any miracle," she stated emphatically.

I didn't want to stay where I wasn't wanted, but I also didn't want to leave until I figured out what was going on. I managed to remain in the house for ten more days, during which time I had long conversations with her two children, several close friends, and her therapist. None of them were encouraging. I was deflated but resigned. We drafted a separation agreement and were formally divorced six months later.

The morning after the agreement was signed, I drove a packed carload of my stuff down to Knotts Island and moved into the apartment above the Tillerys' garage. It became my home, thanks to Nancy and Terry's abundant generosity, for the next year.

Shortly after the move, I drove ninety minutes north to the VA Medical Center in Hampton, Virginia. While I waited, they transferred my medical records down from Washington and assigned me a primary-care physician and psychiatrist. The VA Medical Centers (unlike the Department of Veterans Affairs) had by that time been fully computerized, which greatly enhanced its efficiency. I got bloodwork done that day and scheduled an appointment with the physician for the following week.

When I returned, he checked my vitals, reviewed my lab results, and gave me a physical exam. Once he had finished, he looked over and asked me if I was aware that I had diabetes. It was news to me. He showed me the numbers and asked that I have the tests redone to be sure that there hadn't been an error. I walked down the hall, had another blood test, and returned the following week for the results. The diagnosis was the same—type-II diabetes.

"Were you exposed to Agent Orange while you were in Vietnam?" the doctor asked.

"Exposed to it?" I laughed. "I walked through clouds of it. We all did during the spring of 1968, when the spraying was heaviest along the DMZ. We drank it. We slept on it. We inhaled it."

"Have you had any other symptoms that you are aware of?" he asked.

I told him about the sores that had first appeared while I was in Vietnam.

"Were they biopsied?" he continued.

"Yes," I said. "Several times. I was told that the VA wasn't accepting Agent Orange claims. Besides," I continued, "the statute of limitations for claims expired decades ago."

"That's all changed," he said. "Today's VA is a far cry from the one you guys had to fight with when you first got home. First, there is no more one-year limitation on war zone–related claims. It is also now incumbent on the VA to prove that your ailments *weren't* caused by Agent Orange instead of the other way around.

"No kidding …" I responded. I didn't know what else to say. "What does this all mean?"

After explaining what type-II diabetes was and how it could be traced to my exposure to Agent Orange, he said, "It means that you can file a claim with the Veterans Benefit Administration. They will then arrange for an exam with a private physician to verify these results. In all likelihood, you will receive a 20 percent disability for the diabetes."

I didn't know what to think. On one hand, my monthly disability payment was going to rise. On the other hand, I had diabetes. I didn't like the tradeoff. I was now concerned about my long-term health. The detritus from my time in Vietnam had not only occupied my head but apparently had long been festering inside of the rest of my body as well.

Proving a disability caused by Agent Orange had been nearly impossible since the first victims had returned from the war four decades earlier. Now, after years of denial by the United States government and the manufacturers, there was growing proof that it was the cause of a wide range of ailments. While this allowed the VA to begin providing much-needed care and financial support to thousands of returnees, it was too late for those who had already died because of their exposure.

In that context, my diabetes didn't seem like such a terrible fate. I was, after all, alive.

As soon as I got home, I called Terry and told him the news. I then sent an email out to our growing list of Vietnam buddies. Things were changing for the better at the VA.

CHAPTER 29

November 2007, Albuquerque, New Mexico

My first grandchild, Margaret, was born on November 10, 2007, in Hong Kong. It was the 232nd birthday of the United States Marine Corps. It was also the seventy-first birthday of Bill Negron. Terry Tillery, Dan Burton, Mac Mecham, and perhaps seventy-five more of us were gathered for a First Battalion Fourth Marines reunion dinner in an Albuquerque hotel ballroom. It was the first time that Bill, our Skipper, and Terry, his radio operator, had seen each other since Vietnam.

Shortly before the main course was served, Bill turned to Terry. "Remember that afternoon at the Washout," he asked, matter-of-factly, "when you shot that girl with the backpack of explosives who was crawling under the wire?"

"I didn't shoot her, *you* shot her," Terry countered.

I vaguely remembered the sapper incident because it had occurred in front of my fighting hole. In broad daylight, we had watched as a female North Vietnamese soldier wearing a backpack began to slither under the wire near the outer edge of the perimeter. We assumed that the backpack contained a bomb. I don't recall feeling any great sense of urgency. She was moving slowly and, frankly, we couldn't believe what we were seeing. Terry and several others were nearby. Bill Negron came over to get a closer look.

"Should I shoot?" I asked. She was lined up in my rifle sights.

All I recall after that was the explosion. We'd all ducked for cover.

Back at the reunion dinner, Bill looked over at Terry and reconsidered. "Okay, yeah, well maybe I did shoot her. I don't know. But I do remember the explosion. Bullet must have hit her in the backpack. Bits of her body and uniform were flying all over the place. Remember that? What a fuckin' mess."

"My God!" The comment came from one of the wives. "Do you two have any idea what you are talking about? You are arguing about who *shot* someone." She quickly got up from the table and left the room.

The rest of us watched her leave, then shrugged as we blankly looked back at each other.

"What's up with her?" Terry asked to no one in particular.

After dinner, a raffle drawing was held. The prize was a baby quilt that had been hand-sewn by the wife of one of our buddies. At its center was a Marine Corps emblem framed on three sides by the colored battle ribbons earned by Vietnam combat veterans. The stitching at the top read, *Charlie 1/4.* I hoped that one of my raffle tickets would win the quilt for my new granddaughter.

Terry won the drawing. He walked to the dais, was handed the quilt, and returned to his chair. After sitting quietly for several minutes as the speeches continued, he got up, walked around to where Bill was sitting, knelt beside him, and placed the quilt on his lap.

"Happy Birthday, Skipper," he whispered.

I had watched the whole scene unfold. While mildly disappointed, I was moved by Terry's thoughtful gesture. Several moments later, out of the corner of my eye, I saw Bill rise from his chair and walk around the table in my direction. With the quilt in his hands, he knelt beside me.

"Happy birthday, Margaret," he whispered as he placed the quilt on my lap.

Bill Negron had been a seminal figure to me in the sixteen years since we had found each other. I loved having him in my life and treasured these rare occasions when we were able to spend time together. His breathing sounded more labored, but his spirit and sense of humor remained intact. I knew, both from our conversations and from speaking with his wife, Myrna, that he continued to struggle with PTSD. She told me about a recent incident at a local hospital when, while coming out of anesthesia after a surgical procedure on his left arm, he viciously attacked five hospital staff members with his right arm, convinced that they were North Vietnamese soldiers who had come to get him.

Bill was the one person who could look into my soul and see all that was so deeply tangled within. We had come together at a time when both of us were wrestling with the demons of our past and searching for something—anything—to hold on to. We found each other. I remembered my amazed reaction to the first email that I received from him with the handle, *c14actual* the radio call sign for the commanding officer of C Company, First Battalion, Fourth Marines. I thought of all the conflicts that this man had endured. He'd been a professional boxer in Madison Square Garden, a mercenary at Cuba's Bay of Pigs, and a survivor of three combat tours in Vietnam, where he had received a Silver Star, two Bronze Stars, and three Purple Hearts. And yet, after all of that and certainly more, the defining moment of his life, as articulated by his email handle, had been, like mine, the three days that we survived on LZ Loon. Of course, he understood me.

In February 2009, Bill sent me an email that graphically illustrated the still-tortured state of his mind.

> There isn't a day goes by that I don't think about smoking my pistol. Whenever I'm down and thinking the world sucks, one or two of the guys I lost in the war stop by to visit me. Someday I will join them, and I'll be young again. Semper Fi.

Through his emails and our phone conversations, Bill evoked the enduring residual horror that had occupied a permanent residence in his soul since Loon. I shared much of it myself, but rarely with the crippling intensity that he lived with every day. Over time, while his breathing continued to deteriorate, his mental health did improve. Our recoveries shared several of the same elements: the passage of time, counseling and medications from the VA, and the sweet words, "another brother found."

As our numbers grew, so did our strength. Charlie Company was, indeed, coming together again.

CHAPTER 30

2008–2009, Fort Lee, New Jersey

After five years of writing *Loon: A Marine Story*, Random House agreed to publish the manuscript. I was thrilled and relieved. My life was about to change dramatically for the better. The publishing date was set for May 2009.

In September 2008, after a year of solitary living in Nancy and Terry's Knotts Island garage, I moved into an apartment in Fort Lee, New Jersey, that was owned by my daughter Sarah's in-laws. The contrast to Knotts Island was palpable. I went from being thirty miles from the nearest grocery store to a perch that was five floors above the inbound toll booths of the George Washington Bridge. I was now closer to family, friends, and Random House. The New York area would also be a convenient launching pad for the book tour that would begin after *Loon*'s publication.

In early October, I drove to the East Orange VA Medical Center and presented myself. With a minimum of paperwork, my medical records were again transferred, and I was assigned a primary-care physician and a psychiatrist. Lab tests were done and appointments with the doctors were made for the following week. After receiving a tour of the facility, I felt that I was again in good hands. When I met my new physician, he reviewed my lab results, gave me a physical exam, and asked if there had been any significant changes to my diet or exercise routine since my last exam.

"No," I responded, "but I did move up here from North Carolina recently and got out of the habit of checking my blood every day."

While looking down at my chart, he said, "It appears that your sugar level has spiked since your last exam. There could be many reasons for this, diet and exercise being chief among them. How is the feeling in your fingers and toes?" he inquired.

"My fingers and toes?" I responded. I wiggled my toes inside of my socks and gently rubbed the fingers of each hand back and forth against my thumbs.

"Yes," he said, reaching for my right hand, "do you have feeling in your fingers and toes?"

"Some better than others," I responded. Several of my fingers were always numb, particularly when it was cold. My toes usually tingled, but I never gave it much attention.

He began a deliberate process of checking the feeling and mobility in each of my fingers and toes. When he was finished, he looked up at me and said, "You're ten for ten. You've lost some or all feeling and response in every one of them."

"What does that mean?" I asked.

"Here's how it works," he replied. "The VA will contact you shortly to set up a consult with an outside physician to confirm the results. If she agrees with the findings, you can file for an increase to your disability. Since you are now getting 20 percent for the diabetes, your rating will increase to 40 percent—that's 1 percent for each affected digit."

"Wow," I said, while quickly trying to do the math in my head.

He then continued, "How's your sex life?"

The question caught me off guard. I was still thinking about my fingers and toes. "Sex life?" I responded. Really? I paused to consider the question. "Could be better, Doc. How's yours?" I asked. Then I laughed. He appeared to be about ten years older than I and was wearing a wedding ring.

"I've been married for thirty-six years. So far so good." He smiled. "What do you mean yours could be better?"

"Well, I was half kidding," I said. "There's no one currently in my life, but my performance has waned considerably in recent years."

He went on to explain. "The diabetes-caused neuropathy that has restricted the blood flow to your fingers and toes also affects the blood flow to your penis. Unfortunately, the VA does not consider your penis to be a digit. That's the bad news. The good news is that, as a malfunctioning creative organ, the VA will provide you with Viagra, at no charge, and add a modest stipend to your disability compensation."

Creative organ? So, the VA even had a sense of humor.

Not long after I moved to Fort Lee in the fall of 2008, several of us received an email from Thurm Moore, the keeper of the website for the First Battalion Fourth Marines. In it, he attached a recent posting that he had downloaded from the message board. He added the comment, "Figured one of you guys might have known this kid's dad."

> I *am trying to find anybody that might have served with my father Thomas J. Morrissey Jr. He was with C Company, 1st Battalion, 4th Marines, 3rd Marine Division. He was killed on June 5, 1968. Please call me at the number below anytime. Thank you.*
>
> *Thomas J. Morrissey III*

I sat in stunned silence as I read and reread the posting.

"Thomas J. Morrissey III."

As I said his name out loud, the memory of his father washed over me. I thought of Norma—his mother and my friend Tom's widow. The war was not over for either of them. Beneath the website posting, there was a number with a Massachusetts area code. I took a breath, picked up the phone, and thus began a five-year journey that would change the lives of three Vietnam War survivors forever.

The voice that answered was his father's—same cadence, same New England accent. I identified myself and was transported back into the presence of that wonderful twenty-year-old boy. I was momentarily speechless.

"Jack? Hey Jack, are you there?" Tom asked.

"Yes, I'm here, Tom," I replied after several long seconds. "Sorry. You sound like your father. Your voice could be your father's voice." I told him that I'd seen his posting on the battalion website and that I was calling because I had known his father.

"He was a remarkable person—a wonderful guy," I said. "I was there when he died," I caught myself. I regretted bringing up the subject of his father's death so abruptly. The image of Tom lying dead on the hilltop flashed into my mind. What if his son asked me for details? What would I say?

"That's great, Jack. I'm glad you called," he replied. "I just heard from one other guy who knew him. I can't remember his name. I'm not good with names. He said he was there and that he was wounded in the battle. Woody, that was his name."

"Wayne Wood?" I asked.

"Yeah, that's the guy," Tom said. "I think he was from Iowa or someplace out that way."

"That's great," I replied. "Wayne was a machine gunner like

your father. It was a bad day for machine gunners." That was a stupid thing to say, I thought, but we had lost four machine gunners during the attack and had missed their combat presence as the battle raged for another day. "He was injured by the same round that killed your dad."

I told him that I had made several references to his dad in my forthcoming book, *Loon: A Marine Story*. "I also have pictures that I took of your dad," I said. "Good pictures." Tom had been my favorite subject. Whether he was walking by my hole or eating a can of C-rations, I could rarely resist taking a photo of him. He was the epitome of cool.

"Yeah, I have a few pictures that he sent back, but not much else," Tom replied. "You know, the telegram and a letter from the guy who was head of the company."

"Bill Negron?" I asked.

"I think so," Tom replied. "I haven't looked at that stuff in a long time."

"Where are you, Tom? Is this a Massachusetts number?" I asked.

"Yes," he replied. "We live south of Boston, near the Rhode Island border."

"Are you married? Do you have a family?" I continued.

"I am married," he responded. "My wife's name is Jen. We have two kids. Our daughter, Katelin, is in the tenth grade and our son, Thomas, is in seventh."

"Thomas? Thomas the fourth?" I asked almost incredulously.

"Yes. He's named after me. Well, mostly he's named after his grandfather."

My friend Tom was not forgotten. He was very much alive—two more generations alive. Tom went on to tell me an abbreviated story of his life. I interrupted with a question or a comment, but mostly encouraged him to keep talking. He told me that he had been raised by his father's parents, Lorraine and Thomas Sr., in Dover where he had been born and later in Middletown, Rhode Island, where he lived in a houseful of seven older aunts and uncles. A good athlete, he'd been a professional jai alai player at a time when the sport was growing in popularity in South Florida and southern New England, because of the gaming revenue that it generated. It is an indoor sport of Basque derivation in which a small, hard ball is played off the walls of an enclosed court with a handheld basket.

He went on to tell me that he worked nights for a food distributor north of Boston—a long commute. He had a second job as an independent painter/contractor. I liked him. He sounded like a son that his father would be proud of. Throughout the call, I waited for him to mention his mother. Thrilled as I was to be speaking with him, I could not get Norma out of my mind.

"Tom," I asked as our call was concluding, "do you know your mother?"

"No," he quickly replied, "I don't know my mother."

"Don't know her?" I stammered.

"No," he said. "As I told you, I was raised by my grandparents."

Tom and I would not speak again for four years.

After the call ended, I felt a mixture of joy and relief. Tom sounded like a good guy and seemed to be doing well. He was happily married, had a growing family and a good job. Did I still care about finding Norma? Having found her son, it no longer seemed that important.

But still, I couldn't get her out of my mind.

CHAPTER 31

2009, Washington, DC and Fort Lee

In early May 2009, I drove down to Arlington National Cemetery to attend the interment ceremony for three of our marines who had been killed in a helicopter crash during our evacuation from LZ Loon. Terry Tillery was also there, having driven up from North Carolina. Their remains had been recovered from the site—now overgrown jungle—the previous year. I was moved to know that there were dedicated teams of people working in Vietnam to locate and identify those remains that could be recovered. Having lost forty boys during the battle, it was deeply emotional for us to finally see three of them buried with full military honors. Decades before, while Terry and I had still been in Vietnam, thirty-seven similar ceremonies had taken place throughout the United States.

It was a dizzying period for me. While writing the book, I had relived the battle in solitude every day for seven years. Now, within several short weeks, I had spoken with Thomas J. Morrissey III, whose father had been killed on Loon, and attended the interment ceremony for three boys who had died during the evacuation. It was a lot of LZ Loon after forty years.

Three weeks later, on May 19, 2009, *Loon: A Marine Story* was published. All that had been so intensely personal for so long was now out there for all to read. The book was received favorably by both civilian and military reviewers. *The Washington Times* called it, "A remarkable odyssey ... insightful, haunting, extraordinary." Brigadier General Thomas Draude, USMC (Ret.), writing for the US Naval Institute's *Proceedings*, called it, "a delight to read."

Having lived alone with my memories, it was disorienting to walk into Barnes & Noble bookstore and see a stack of my books featured on the "New Releases" table by the front door. I also noted that it was filed alphabetically by author in the Vietnam War section next to, *In Retrospect: The Tragedy and Lessons of Vietnam*, by Robert S. McNamara, the very architect of war. Six weeks after publication, *Loon: A Marine Story* was the best-selling amazon.com book in the category of Vietnam Biographies and Memoirs. It also made the bestseller lists of the *Boston Globe* and the *Denver Post*. I never could have imagined such an outcome on that July evening in 2002 when I began to transcribe my letters home.

The writing and publication of *Loon: A Marine Story* was uplifting. Reliving my Marine Corps training and Vietnam combat experience had helped me to excise the lingering horrors that I had long buried. I allowed myself to be proud of my service without the anxiety, guilt, and shame that had dogged me for decades. I felt that I was recovering. It was apparent from the start that I had tapped into something. I received emails and letters from Vietnam veterans, their children, and mothers who now had nineteen-year-old sons of their own. I received hundreds of supportive comments, including one from the commandant of the Marine Corps in Washington, DC. They continue to this day. I am gratified that, in pursuing my own recovery, I contributed to that of so many others.

Over the next year, I traveled around the country promoting the book. Throughout, former Charlie Company comrades appeared in varying states of physical and emotional health. Some called in to radio shows. Others appeared in person at book events. It could be agonizing to listen as their own recollections of those three days on LZ Loon bore out. Several said it was the first time they had ever spoken of the battle. Each had a story. Mine was but one. I still thought of Tom Morrissey. A humorous passage that I'd written about him was one of my favorites to read at book events. I also thought about his son. I'd hoped that he'd be proud to see his dad's name in print. I might have called him again but had misplaced his phone number. Perhaps our paths would cross again someday.

Five months after *Loon: A Marine Story* was published, I received an email from Glenn Benjaminsen. He said that he had read the book and noted my friendship with his cousin Sid MacLeod. While he had never known Sid, he said that Sid Sr. was his great uncle. He went on to tell me that, since he'd been a child, Sid's framed Marine Corps portrait had hung prominently in his grandmother's house. Whenever he looked at it, Glenn wondered what Sid's life might have been like had he lived.

I visited Glenn and his wife Kathy at their Massachusetts home several months later. Sid just came alive. Glenn told me that they had driven down to visit Sid's father several times in Virginia and spent hours going through his memorabilia. I told him story after story about Sid and our time together before going to Vietnam. He was a superbly rare friend. I still miss him. I shall forever be indebted to Glenn and Kathy for bringing him back into my life. I loved knowing that Sid's memory was being held in such capable and loving hands.

That fall, I spoke to a group of students at Asnuntuck Community College in Enfield, Connecticut. When I arrived, I was met at the door by a security guard who appeared to be about my age. He knew that I was coming and addressed me by name. Without fanfare, he led me down the hall to the office of my host. Several hours later, after the speech, after the lunch, and after a lingering session with several students, the security guard quietly entered the room and stood patiently by the door until the conversations had concluded. He then walked over to me, extended his arms, and held me in a long embrace. When he let go and looked at me, I could see that his cheeks were streaked with tears. "Frank Thompson," he whispered in my ear. "I was with Bravo 1/7 in 1968. *Semper fi*, brother. Welcome home."

I was momentarily taken aback, although not surprised by the encounter. "Thanks, brother. Welcome home to you," I replied. "You doing okay?"

"Yeah," he replied. "I got this job nine years ago. They treat me well. I heard part of your speech. I was standing in the back. We were in Nam about the same time. I wanted to thank you for keeping our story alive."

The two of us stood wordlessly arm in arm for several seconds.

"What is it about you marines, anyway?' The question came from Russ Thomas, a childhood friend who lived nearby and had come over for the event. "Any time I see two of you together," he continued, "it's like you've always known each other."

Together, Frank and I turned, looked at each other, and smiled. Indeed. We had.

It was an unfeigned moment. The pride that I had long ago lost in being a United States Marine had returned in recent years thanks to Terry, the others that gathered at Knotts Island earlier that spring, and the steady stream of our former brothers-in-arms who continued to emerge from the darkness beyond. Although Asnuntuck's Frank Thompson and I had not served together in Vietnam, we shared that same bond.

There is a saying, "Once a marine, always a marine." Our brotherhood would never let us forget that, even if, for thirty years, I had tried so hard to.

CHAPTER 32

July 2010, Sanford, Maine

On February 4, 2010, I returned home after several weeks away to find a stack of unanswered mail and unread email messages. I decided to start with the emails. After a quick scan, one stood out like a flower in the desert.

Hello Jack,

I found your email address on your blog.

I also purchased your book. I enjoyed it immensely. You brought closure to a lot of questions that I have been living with for many years.

With respect and thanks for serving our country.

Norma Morrissey

(Wife of Tom Morrissey)

When I wrote Norma back the next morning, I told her how glad I was to hear from her, expressed my long-belated condolences for her loss, and let her know how profoundly her late husband's death had affected all of us. I included several pictures of him that I had taken. I also told her that several of us had spoken with her son after seeing his post on the battalion website.

While overjoyed to have heard from her, I was at a loss as to what I should do next. Questions rose in my mind, but I wasn't sure if I wanted the answers. I did, however, continue to wonder how she and her son had been separated. My curiosity did not linger for long. Norma wrote back later that day. While putting some of my questions to rest, she opened a Pandora's box of others. She remembered her late husband as vividly as if he had just left the room.

> *Tom was the love of my life. I have yet to meet anyone who compares to him. It is funny how my memories make me feel like it was only yesterday. Every time I smell a Zippo lighter, I think of Tom. When I see Ray-Ban aviator sunglasses, I think of Tom. He is still a part of me.*

She went on to share what she referred to as, "A brief synopsis of my crazy life."

> *Tom's parents were against our relationship. They interfered continually. They tried to get our marriage annulled. From the day Tom left for*

Camp Pendleton they harassed me. In one of Tom's last letters, he said that he was going to write to his mother and tell her to back off. He was pissed.

It was a hard time in my life and Tom's. He did not need that. He had enough to deal with being in Vietnam.

I left young Tom with my mother so that I could try to find a place for us to get away from my in-laws. While I was gone, my mother-in-law took my son from my mother for the afternoon promising that she'd have him back by dinnertime. She did not ever bring him back.

I could write a book and cry an ocean, but I will spare you.

Fast forward …

Obviously, my son has been lied to throughout the years. There are two sides to every story. It is such a shame that he will never know either of his birth parents. I ache to see him. I hope that I will before I die.

I am happy that you were in contact with my son, Tom. I am sure he had many questions that needed to be answered. Thank you from the bottom of my heart.

I was in another relationship after Tom. I have two sons aged thirty-six and thirty-nine.

We had a thriving furniture, retail and auction business which we've recently sold.

I am living alone in Sanford, Maine.

Thank you for being such a good friend to my husband. He deserved to have a friend like you. Thank you for getting back to me and, once again, thank you for the photos.

I wish you the best of luck in all your future endeavors.

God Bless

What exactly had happened forty-one years ago? I would never know. I wasn't there. But I now knew why my friend Tom had not been himself in the weeks before he was killed and had requested emergency home leave.

Over the next several months, Norma and I worked our way into each other's lives. We became Facebook friends and exchanged emails. We kept it simple. I liked having her in my life. It gave me a sense of peace and some closure. It was clear that she wanted to reunite with her son but seemed resigned to the fact that it would probably never happen. That spring, I asked if I could come visit her in the summer. She leapt at the offer, invited me for lunch, and said that she would like to have her sister Debra join us.

In early June 2010, Roz invited me to spend a week at her cottage in Maine at a time when our daughters would be visiting. I happily accepted. I thought back to her first such invitation in July 1972 that had led to our reconciliation and marriage a week later. While there would be no repeat of that happy ending, Roz continued to be the same gracious woman with whom I had long ago fallen in love. In recent years, we spoke and emailed, usually to share stories about our three daughters. The girls had all graduated from college. Sarah, married and mother to Margaret and now Mason, was teaching at a bilingual independent school in Hong Kong. Martha was successfully launching her career in the fashion industry across the Hudson River from me in New York City. Sylvia, also married and mother to new son Alden, was teaching children with autism in Davis, California, while her husband completed his graduate studies.

The week in Maine passed peacefully. Much of our attention focused on the perpetual activity of our three small grandchildren and my dog, Charlie, a frisky miniature schnauzer puppy I had recently rescued. Days were spent reading, walking, and avoiding all temptation to plunge into the frigid North Atlantic Ocean. Evenings were spent on the porch, watching the tide come in and go out, laughing, telling family stories, and avoiding mosquitoes. We drove the boat to Boothbay Harbor to buy ice-cream cones, saltwater taffy, and tourist trinkets. Along the way, we spotted harbor seals frolicking on the rocks and lobstermen pulling their traps.

Vietnam was far away.

On the morning of July 15, 2010, Charlie and I said our goodbyes and set out on the ninety-minute trip southwest to Sanford for our visit with Norma and her sister, Debra. The drive took us down the Maine coast through the town of Yarmouth, where our young family had lived for five happy years. It had been our home when Sarah presented me with the rubbing of Sid MacLeod's name from the Vietnam Veterans Memorial. We then passed through downtown Portland, the site of my early professional posting, which had come at a time when I felt that a long and successful business career was assured.

As I approached Sanford, I could see that it resembled dozens of other old New England mill towns. First settled in 1739 at the end of the French and Indian Wars, it grew throughout the nineteenth century. Manufacturers were attracted by the power potential of the Mousam River. Like Dover, thirty-three miles to the south, it soon developed into a center of textile manufacturing. Then, in a pattern that was repeated throughout the mill towns of the Northeast in the mid-twentieth century, the looms were either shut down or moved to the south in search of cheaper labor. As a result, thousands of workers were left unemployed, and many of the enormous brick manufacturing buildings were razed or abandoned.

On this Saturday morning, the town looked vibrant. I drove past several of the old brick mills, crossed the Mousam River, and continued up the hill on the other side. Within a mile, I turned left on Norma's street and began looking at mailbox numbers. Unlike my first attempt to find her forty-two years earlier, I had a name and address and was assured of a warm welcome. Her house was a simple blue ranch, set back about halfway down on the right. I parked in the driveway, let Charlie out to stretch and pee, and walked across the lawn to the front door.

The woman who appeared from within was lovely and bore a calm, peaceful demeanor. Norma stood about five feet three inches tall, had shoulder-length gray hair, and a face that radiated welcoming warmth. My mind flashed back forty-two years to the girl in the grainy photo that her late husband carried in his side pocket. She had an expression through which the years evaporated into a swirl of long-dormant memories and new possibilities. Debra, broadcasting the same sweet countenance, was by her side. She leaned over and gently patted Charlie, which calmed him right down.

Norma's home was neat and tidy. There were pictures on the walls, doilies on the tabletops, and keepsakes throughout. As we entered the living room, my eye was drawn to a framed photograph of a lovely, dark-haired teenaged girl that sat on a shelf to the left. I briefly wondered who she was. While I took it all in, Norma went into the kitchen and returned with a pitcher of lemonade and three glasses, which she placed on the coffee table. She then motioned for me to have a seat on the sofa. She and Debra sat in adjacent chairs. Any misgivings I may have had about meeting Norma or visiting her home evaporated the instant I crossed the threshold. This was more than a mere courtesy call. It was a life event that had been four decades in the making.

After some small talk, we wove our way back to the awful summer of 1968 when her husband was killed in Vietnam and her fourteen-month-old son was taken from her. We then retreated further to a snowy afternoon in February 1965 when, sitting in the back seat of Barry Bittner's car with her friend Peggy in the front passenger seat, Norma first spotted Tom Morrissey driving his mother's white station wagon through downtown Dover.

As she spoke, Debra injected an occasional anecdote, as I listened in rapt silence. There were times when her story was punctuated with exquisitely painful detail. At other times, however, the far-off memories had been long since put to rest. After recounting their courtship, Norma went out to the kitchen and returned with a plate of sandwiches, a bowl of potato chips, more lemonade, napkins, and a plate of cookies, which she placed on the coffee table. As we ate, she continued in an almost trancelike state.

On that Saturday afternoon in Sanford, it was clear to me that Norma and Debra were far from recovered. Tom's death and the awful events that ensued continued to cause deep pain in both women. I had been so absorbed, over the years, in thinking about myself and the other veterans, living and dead, with whom I had served, that I had given little thought to "they who also serve"—the 58,220 families of the fallen. The war was over for me, but it was still being fought in real time for them. Many parents of the dead and wounded had died by this time. The widows, however, like Norma; children, like Tom Morrissey III; aunts, like Debra; and brothers, sisters, cousins, classmates, and former next-door neighbors still bore the searingly sad memory of that proud young person who went off to war and never returned.

Norma was not alone in her grief. Seventeen thousand five hundred thirty-nine of the dead had been married, with an estimated twenty-two thousand children. The average age of those fighting in Vietnam was twenty-two years old, four years younger than any fighting force that this country had ever sent off to war. This meant that most of them didn't live long enough to marry. Those who did, married young women who were probably close in age to Norma. Theirs is a heart-breaking story of freshly planted young love that never had the opportunity to fully flower. Each of these widows endured their own horrific "We regret to inform you …" moment, when two uniformed representatives from her husband's service branch arrived at the front door to deliver the dreadful news.

Vietnam War widows received much of the same public treatment as returning Vietnam veterans. In the late 1960s, the country was polarized by the war. While many Americans unfairly equated those who had served in the military with support for the war, there was no convenient political or social slot into which the widows might comfortably fit. Some of them felt that they were shunned by the American public for the sin of having married a man who had fought and died for his country. The Veterans Administration, Veterans Service Organizations, and our country treated them with the same ambivalence as they did the returning Vietnam veterans. This lingers as an unspoken shame of our Vietnam experience. Many Vietnam War widows went on to suffer from the symptoms of PTSD, just as if they had been on the battlefield on the day their husbands were killed.

Vietnam War widows were old enough to remember President John F. Kennedy's funeral on Monday, November 25, 1963. The funeral cortege had proceeded from the United States Capitol to the White House, to St. Matthew's Cathedral in Washington, DC, and across the Potomac River to the Arlington National Cemetery. President Johnson had declared it to be a National Day of Mourning. Schools and businesses were closed so that the nation could watch the procession on live television. Few eyes could divert themselves from President Kennedy's widow, Jacqueline, the most admired woman in America at the time.

From the moment of her departure from the White House on foot, to her cathedral entrance and exit, until the presentation of the folded American flag from her husband's coffin hours later, her stoically dignified bearing provided the entire country with an example of how to grieve. Throughout the day, Mrs. Kennedy, a widow for only three days, displayed no outward evidence of her grief to the public.

Brief years later, each of these Vietnam War widows would sit at her own husband's graveside, as a military honor guard fired a salute and a uniformed soldier knelt before her to present the American flag from *her* husband's coffin. Some later wrote of remembering Jackie at that moment. They, too, tried not to cry, as they kept their own crushing grief self-contained and publicly hidden.

As the afternoon wore on, the words began to blur in my mind—Middletown, Bangor, Dover, the prom night, Tom's family, Norma's family, their marriage, her pregnancy, and Tom's Vietnam orders. I knew that there were gaps in my understanding. It was a complex story. Some of the facts were forever etched in Norma's memory. Most had come out in her email and in the first twenty minutes of my visit.

She remembered the good times, but many of the bad ones had been lost to her grief decades before. The entire relationship, from the moment that she first saw Tom from the back of Barry Bittner's car on Main Street, until the day that he was killed in Vietnam, had lasted thirty months. Occasionally, I'd push for an additional detail, and she'd respond, "You know, Jack, it was a long time ago. There are some things I don't remember so well."

By late afternoon, it was time to begin my drive home to New Jersey. I rose, Charlie scurried, and Norma led me across the room toward the side door. On the way, I paused in front of the framed photograph of the teenaged girl that had caught my eye when I first arrived. I'd been glancing at it over Norma's shoulder all day.

"Who's that?" I asked.

"Oh," she replied, "that's my granddaughter, Katelin."

"Your granddaughter?" I was still trying to sort out her family ties.

"Yes," she went on, "my son Tom's daughter. I have a grandson too, Thomas the Fourth."

We had spoken little of her son or his family because there was little known about their lives, other than what I'd gleaned from my conversation with him the year before.

"But … you don't know them," I continued.

"No, I don't," she replied, "but Katelin has a Facebook page. I can't 'friend' her, of course, but every time she changes her profile picture, I make a copy and put it in that frame."

"And Thomas …?" I asked.

"He doesn't have a Facebook page. I don't know what he looks like. He'd be fourteen years old. Katelin is sixteen."

We continued into the kitchen as I tried to digest yet another wrenching piece of the puzzle. It had been an exhausting day. I put Charlie on his leash and headed out the side door onto the deck. I took a moment to admire Norma's backyard gardens. There was a large, fenced-in vegetable garden close to the house that contained ripening tomatoes and rows upon rows of lettuce, peas, beans, and squash. Her perennial garden, in magnificent bloom, was planted beyond the well-trimmed lawn. It was all neat and lovely—the obvious result of her labor and love. Garden-wise, mid-July is as good as it gets during Maine's brief summers.

While Charlie slept peacefully beside me in the passenger seat, I passed the six-hour drive reflecting on the day. I thought about how welcome Norma had made me feel as she ushered me from one long-ago memory to the next. I thought about Debra and all that she had endured at such a young age. I thought about the lush gardens. My abiding memory, however, was the picture of her granddaughter, Katelin. It stayed in my mind all the way home, into the next day, and for years to come.

I was glad that Norma had found me. Having now spent the day in her home, I felt that I was sending my friend Tom a message that his wife and her younger sister were, for the most part, thriving.

I decided to be happy. Lives go on. Mine certainly had.

Jack McLean & Norma Morrissey

CHAPTER 33

2009, Fort Lee

On the afternoon of December 12, 2009, while driving home from an appointment at the VA Medical Center in East Orange, I decided to stop by the Newark office of the VVA. I was grateful for the help that their Washington office had given me when I filed my disability claim, so thought I would introduce myself to their local representative. As with most VSOs, they were housed in the same building as the regional VA. When I got to the seventh-floor office, the door was locked. I tried knocking.

"Hang on a minute, I'm on the phone," the female voice came from within.

After waiting outside for several minutes, I heard approaching footsteps, and the door was swung open.

"Well …?" she asked. I was face to face with a sturdy middle-aged woman with a full head of graying dark hair. She had the well-seasoned look of someone who had been through a few battles herself.

"Is this the VVA?" I asked hesitantly.

"Who wants to know?" she snapped back with a slight smile while ushering me in. "Take a seat over there," she said, pointing to a worn chair sitting in front of a well-ordered metal desk. A corkboard on the adjacent wall was covered with snapshots of soldiers, military unit insignias, inspirational cards, and all manner of personal and professional paraphernalia.

"Who were you with?" she asked after settling herself in behind the desk.

"Excuse me?" The question caught me off guard.

"Army, navy? You know, what branch of the service were you in?" she clarified.

"Oh," I responded, "Marine Corps. First Battalion, Fourth Marines, Third Division. I was in Charlie Company."

"So, you were a grunt," she said. It wasn't a question.

"Yes, ma'am."

"My name is Margaret. You were lucky to find me. I was about to leave for the day. I'm only here a few days a week."

"I'm Jack."

"You divorced?"

Surprised, I responded, "Yes. Twice. How did you know?"

"Not a big leap, Jack. Most of you guys are divorced. You got a VA disability?"

"Yes. Thirty percent PTSD, fifty percent from Agent Orange."

"You got a job?"

"No." Then I caught myself and continued, "Well, I'm a writer. I wrote a book."

"Good for you," she said without enthusiasm before continuing. "When was the last time you had a *real* job?"

I thought for a few seconds. "Four or five years ago, I'd say."

"And ..."

I wasn't sure where this was going or why she suddenly seemed so interested in my background when, minutes before, she'd said that she was headed out the door. I took a breath and proceeded to recite the highlights of my recent life.

"Twice married and divorced. Five jobs in nine years. Should I keep going?"

"What kind of jobs?"

"Two were corporate, three were with nonprofits. I quit looking after the last one and started writing full time."

"So, I'd say that you have had trouble holding down a job.

Would you agree?"

"I did have one for seventeen years once," I said in a weak attempt to defend myself.

"Why did you leave?"

"Because they were assholes." I half laughed.

"And the next five?"

"Same deal," I said without laughing.

There is a VA disability category for unemployability. Having worked for most of my life, I had never considered myself to be unemployable, but most of my recent employers had. Margaret began by explaining that, for me to be considered unemployable, I would have to be 70 percent disabled in at least one category. Since my PTSD disability was 30 percent and my diabetes was 50 percent, I didn't meet the criteria. She explained that the diabetes benefit was maxed and could never go above 50 percent. I would, therefore, need to get my PTSD rating up to 70 percent. I had been given the opportunity to appeal the PTSD ruling when it was awarded but, despite Terry Tillery's urging, decided not to. My window to do so had long since closed. The only way to now have it increased was to make a plea to the Board of Veterans Appeals in Washington, DC. The process, she said, would take years, and the odds of success were slim.

The Board of Veterans Appeals is an administrative tribunal, within the Department of Veterans Affairs, that acts as the ultimate arbiter for veterans' benefits disputes. The chairman is appointed by the president and confirmed by the Senate. There is no limit to the number of attorneys who sit on the board. Each is nominated by the secretary of veterans affairs and confirmed by the Senate. At the end of 2015, the board was composed of sixty-three lawyers.

Because my circumstances had changed significantly since my original PTSD claim was filed in 2005, I felt I had a reasonable shot at getting my rating increased. One of the criteria for having it raised to 70 percent was "demonstrated unemployability." That meant proving that I was unable to "maintain substantially gainful employment as a result of service-connected disabilities." Given my recent experience, this seemed achievable.

Margaret and I decided to go forward. We completed the paperwork, which she would later file with the Newark office of the Veterans Benefit Administration downstairs. As I left her office, her final words were, "Don't even call me for at least two years. When I hear something, one way or the other, I'll let you know." I paused, nodded, and headed for the elevators. Two years?

The Veterans Benefit Administration arm of the Department of Veterans Affairs still operated in the previous century. Like the Veterans Health Administration, it was under well-publicized scrutiny during the 2000s to respond to the needs of the growing horde of new veterans who were returning from Iraq and Afghanistan. It was the largest influx since the Vietnam War had ended, thirty-five years earlier. Unlike the Health Administration, however, the Benefit Administration's records were not computerized. When Margaret told me not to call her about my disability claim for at least two years, she wasn't kidding. Every single benefit claim for every single veteran existed only in one paper file. None was computerized.

Once they received the paperwork from Margaret, the Newark office of the Veterans Benefit Administration would review it, attach the legal case from the VVA lawyers, attach my original PTSD claim file, affix my DD-214 and VA health history, and send it all down to the Veterans Board of Appeals on Vermont Avenue in Washington, DC. The only potential glitch that I could see would be in locating my original PTSD claim file. I had been living in Knotts Island at the time. This meant that the paper file from that claim was located within the DVA regional office in Winston-Salem, North Carolina.

My appeal was filed with the VVA on September 10, 2010. It was received by the DVA downstairs on October 6 and certified on November 23. It was received and docketed by the Veterans Board of Appeals on December 2. So far, so good. On March 15, 2011, I received a copy of the legal case that had been meticulously prepared by the VVA attorneys. My appeal file was now complete—almost. The Newark office was still trying to locate the old North Carolina PTSD claim file.

In late spring of 2011, I arranged to visit Norma again on my way back from our July family gathering in Maine. Several days before the visit, however, she said that she would be unable to meet, due to the sudden illness of a friend. I was disappointed. Now I might not see her for another year, if ever. There were still details of her history that I was missing, but I was less interested in delving back into them and more interested in knowing that she was okay.

In early February 2012, I drove to Newark to see Margaret. Although it had only been seventeen months since we had filed the appeal, I figured I'd give it a shot. When I walked into her office, she was on the phone and barely looked up. After several minutes of standing patiently in front of her desk, she covered the mouthpiece and whispered, "Another year." On my way out, I walked into the Benefit Administration office on the first floor, filled out an inquiry form, sat down, and waited for nearly an hour. I was finally helped by a most sympathetic clerk who, after poking around on her computer for a long time, informed me that my original claim file was still in Winston-Salem and that it had yet to be transferred to Newark. Telling me what I already knew, she informed me that my appeal could not go forward until it was.

I said that I would drive down to Winston-Salem myself and pick it up. I was only half-kidding. When I got home, I wrote a letter to New Jersey United States Senator Robert Menendez. Perhaps I could get his office to intercede on my behalf.

It was worth a shot.

CHAPTER 34

2012, Fort Lee

The following July, after spending a week with my family in Maine, I again drove down to Sanford to visit Norma. It had been two years since our first meeting and three years since I had spoken with her son, Tom.

When Charlie and I arrived, I noticed that there were several other cars in the driveway. We greeted Norma and Debra at the back door and walked into the kitchen. Norma then led me into the living room and introduced me to Debra's longtime friend Jim, their sister Karen, and Karen's husband, Lee. Jim was a US Army Airborne veteran. Lee, a Vietnam veteran, had been fighting a long battle with lymphoma, which had been attributed to his wartime exposure to Agent Orange. Lee and I talked about his cancer and the difficulties that he had endured with the VA while trying to get the medical treatment he required. It had taken dozens of years for his lymphoma to fully present itself. Fortunately, the timeline for claims had been extended and an increasing number of Vietnam-related

Agent Orange ailments like his had since been covered by the VA. He said that he was now receiving excellent treatment from the VA Medical Center in Manchester, New Hampshire.

Several days after we got home, in late July 2012, I drove to the Veterans Benefit Administration office in Newark to see the helpful clerk I had befriended the previous February. When I walked into the office, she was sitting at her computer, right where I'd left her seven months earlier. She looked up and gave me a smile of vague recognition. After I reintroduced myself, she smiled more broadly and asked if I'd had a good summer. I told her that I just returned from Maine. She said that she had recently returned from a family reunion in South Carolina.

Small talk completed, I asked if she could check to see if there had been any change in the status of my appeal.

"Did you get a letter from us?" she asked.

"No." I responded, "I thought I'd stop by and bug you again."

I smiled. She smiled.

"Okay. Let's look and see what we can find," she said.

After ten minutes of scrolling, she said, "I see that you have the support of Senator Menendez. You have friends in high places, Mr. McLean."

Having received no reply to the letter I had sent to my senator the previous spring, I assumed it had joined hundreds of others in the office "to do" pile. I was wrong. Someone in his office *had* followed up on my inquiry. After more scrolling, she found what I had been waiting for. "Oh, here it is," she said as her voice lifted with slight anticipation. "It says here that your file was located in Winston-Salem last month and is on its way here to Newark."

"Wow. No kidding. I can't believe it!" We both smiled. "What happens when it gets here?"

"It will be reviewed by our disability committee. If all is in order, it will be sent to the Appeals Court in Washington, DC, to complete your file."

"How long before they send it to DC?" I asked.

"That depends. The committee meets twice a week, but they are backed up, as you can imagine. They review each file in the order that it comes in. When yours arrives, it will go to the bottom of the pile. At their current pace, it could take them several months to get to it."

Several months? I thought. *Big deal.* The file had finally made it out of Winston-Salem and had the support of Senator Menendez. Now *that* was a big deal!

Six months later, on the morning of March 11, 2013, a photograph on the front page of *The New York Times* caught my eye. It showed a large office floor with piles upon piles of paper file folders teetering precariously on top of every flat surface in the room. The caption identified it as the Veterans Benefit Administration's Winston-Salem regional claims office.

The volume of paper was so great, the accompanying article said, that the local fire marshal had closed the office, because he feared that the floor might collapse under the weight. The photo had been taken by Aaron Glantz, a reporter for *Investigative Reporting*, who had gained access to it through a Freedom of Information Act request.

I stared at the photograph with disbelief. My file had been buried in that same heap only weeks before the picture was taken. If I had driven down to get it, as I had once sardonically proposed, it would have taken me months ... years ... to locate it. The lead editorial in the *Times* that day was headlined, "The Grim Backlog at Veterans Affairs." The piece detailed how the Veterans Benefit Administration had become overwhelmed with paper, due to the influx of Iraq and Afghanistan veterans. It said that waiting times for veterans seeking disability decisions was stretching into years. This did not include the delays at the Veterans Court of Appeals. A major cause, the editorial stated, was that 97 percent of all veterans' disability claims were still filed on paper. Knowing that my file was sitting safely in Newark gave me hope. By now, perhaps it had been reviewed and sent to Washington, DC. Even if, I optimistically told myself, the Appeals Board was only backed up a year, there was a chance that I might hear something by the summer.

With the coming of spring, Norma and I arranged our annual July visit. I briefly considered getting back in touch with her son, Tom, but he had made it clear to me when we'd spoken four years earlier that he had no interest in finding his mother.

He hadn't sounded angry. He'd told me that he had a lot going on in his life and didn't have time for another distraction.

I was concerned that if I did speak with him, I might be wandering into a decades-old situation for which I had no solution and within which I had no business.

CHAPTER 35

July 2013, East Taunton, Massachusetts

On the evening of March 18, 2013, to my complete astonishment, I received a Facebook friend request from Thomas J. Morrissey IV—Norma's grandson. I accepted and opened the following message:

> jack, I'm the son of Tom the third. My mom and dad talked to you several years ago. I just got the book and I'm in the process of reading it. It is overwhelming for my whole family. I'm glad you wrote the book. I got to know what kind of person my grandfather was (a true hero). I was wondering if you had any more pictures of him. I hope to hear from you soon! thomas

At that instant, I knew that the decision had been made for me. After four long decades, it was going to be up to me and only me to bring my friend Tom Morrissey's family back together again. I was excited at the prospect and relished the challenge.

I posted a reply to Thomas's message on Facebook.

> Thomas, Great to hear from you. Thank you for reaching out. I do remember speaking with your dad several years ago, but then lost his number when I wanted to call him back. I have much to tell you and share. Your grandfather was my dear friend once and forever. Jack

After several exchanges, we agreed that I would call him on the following Sunday evening.

Tom III answered the phone when I called. It sounded like his wife, Jennifer and the kids, Katelin and Thomas IV, were huddled around the receiver, not wanting to miss a word. After mutual apologies for losing each other's phone numbers, Tom and I launched into a conversation that lasted well over an hour. I began by telling him that I had come to know his mother during the years since we last spoke.

"She came into my life the same way you did, Tom, because of the book." I didn't want him to think that I was part of some conspiracy. "She's a lovely woman. We've become friends."

My comments drew no response, but I was glad to have been forthcoming from the start. Tom repeated much that he had previously told me about his life. He'd been a good athlete, played professional jai alai, met Jennifer, got married, and had two wonderful children. As the call ended, he invited me to come visit. I suggested early July when I was on my way up to Maine. He agreed, and we set a date. After the call, I went online and ordered a silver memorial bracelet with *Thomas J. Morrissey Jr. June 5, 1968,* to be engraved across the front. When it arrived a week later, I sent it to Thomas IV. He has yet to remove it from his wrist.

Over the following months, I saw regular Facebook postings from Katelin and Thomas. Like their father, both were good athletes. Much of their news had to do with Thomas's passion for basketball and Katelin's success on her high school field hockey team. Katelin was familiar to me, since I had observed her yearly changes inside the photograph frame on Norma's living room shelf. Thomas was familiar as well. Tall and topped with a shock of jet-black hair, he bore an eerie resemblance to his grandfather.

In early July, Charlie and I set out for our annual New England road trip. Our first stop would now be the Morrissey home in Massachusetts. From there we'd go to Maine, visit with my family for a week, and conclude with our day with Norma in Sanford on the way back home. I was excited about meeting Tom and his family. As with my first visit with Norma, I didn't know what to expect, other than a friendly welcome.

The trip north took me across the George Washington Bridge and up I-95 through New York, Connecticut, and Rhode Island. It was a drive I had made dozens of times over the years. When I turned left onto Tom's Road, I began to look at mailbox numbers. It was a nice neighborhood with attractive, newer, well-kept homes. The Morrissey house sat on a rise, about a mile down on the right. The lawn was freshly mowed, and the flowerbeds were in full bloom. I put Charlie on his leash, we stretched and walked up the driveway to the front door. When I rang the bell, I heard a dog bark from inside. Charlie barked in response.

My first impression was that Thomas J. Morrissey III bore no resemblance to his father. I could, however, see some of his mother there. Standing about five feet ten, with receding dark hair, he had a broad smile and a welcoming demeanor. As we wrestled with our dogs, I walked in, stood clear of the closing door, and we hugged as if we'd known each other for years.

I then saw a young woman who looked to be about seventeen. This must be Katelin. She was as tall and as lovely as her photographs. Thomas, towering behind her, had his grandfather's black hair, eyebrows, smile, eyes, and nose. All had skipped his father's generation and gone directly to him. Jennifer, Tom's wife of twenty years and mother of the two children, came walking out of the kitchen, while drying her hands on a dish towel. She smiled warmly.

I was the first person Tom III had met who had known his father in Vietnam. I was a link to the grandfather Katelin and Thomas IV had never known. Two generations of Tom's family stood before me like it was the most normal day ever, which, of course, it wasn't. While the circumstance that brought us together had been filled with pain, this moment was joyful. The five of us were starting down a path that would forever change our lives for the better.

"Welcome to our home," Thomas III said. "We're really glad you came."

"Thanks," I replied. "I'm glad I came too. Thanks for inviting me."

We then walked into the kitchen and settled in around the counter where Jennifer had laid out snacks and drinks.

"I hope you like steak," Tom said, pointing to the barbecue that was just outside the sliding back door.

"You bet," I replied. "I like everything, but you didn't have to go to the trouble."

"No trouble," Tom replied. "You are our honored guest. We really feel fortunate that you are here."

As we settled in, we made small talk about the weather, my drive up from New York, and their lovely home. All the while, we watched with amusement as our two scurrying dogs playfully chased each other around the kitchen. I soon turned my attention to Tom.

"Tom," I began, "you said that you were raised by your grandparents. What was that like?"

"It was okay," he replied. "Pretty normal, I guess. I had seven older aunts and uncles—you know, my father's siblings—so the house was always pretty busy."

"Did you have friends?" I asked. I really wanted to know about his mother but wasn't sure how to broach the topic.

"Yeah," he responded. "I had friends, played sports—pretty much got along with everybody. Like I said, a pretty normal childhood."

He didn't recall when he had become aware that his father was killed in Vietnam. When I finally did ask about his mother, he said that she had never been mentioned by anyone in his family—not for better and not for worse.

"Were you ever curious about her," I asked, "as a child, teenager, or young man?"

"No, not really," he replied, "except maybe a few times in passing, but otherwise no."

He told me that Jennifer's father had once asked him if he had any desire to find his mother. "I told him my life was full enough without adding any additional stress."

Jennifer had also been curious about her whereabouts and welfare and thought that Tom might benefit from finding her, but she knew better than to press the issue.

When it was time for lunch, Tom pulled a plate of steaks out of the refrigerator, carried them to the back patio, and put them on the grill.

"Come on, Jack," he said, "let's move out here."

On cue, Jennifer, Katelin, Thomas III, and I walked out to the patio, where Jennifer had already set out a large spread of food on the picnic table. Charlie scooted outside and romped around their backyard as the steaks sizzled on the grill. I took several dozen posed pictures of everyone. We ate outside at the picnic table and talked about the kids, Tom's working life, and Jennifer's early life. She'd grown up in Rhode Island, the second-generation daughter of Portuguese parents.

Tom worked the late-night shift in a refrigerated supermarket food warehouse north of Boston. His commute was over an hour each way directly through downtown Boston, which often made it tedious. He had started a small painting business on the side that was beginning to generate some additional income. I could tell that he was thoughtful, responsible, attentive to detail, and, like Jen, deeply involved in the lives of their two children.

After lunch, we settled in the living room. Tom produced several albums that contained memorabilia from his father that included snapshots from his youth, a high school portrait, and several of his Vietnam photos and letters home. He took me down to the family room in the basement and showed me a shadow box that contained his father's combat medals.

"You know, Jack," he said, looking at the medals, "every so often, my grandfather would produce what he said was one of my father's medals and give it to me—you know, his Purple Heart, his Bronze Star. 'Here,' he'd say. 'You should have this.' I never knew if they were my father's medals or not. Once he gave me a flag that he said had been on my father's coffin, but I knew, by looking at it, that it couldn't have been. He was like that on lots of stuff. I guess it was the drinking. It was hard for me. Having never known my father, the few scraps of his things that I had were precious."

His grandfather, Thomas Sr., was a heavy drinker and had not been a positive presence in his life. His grandmother, Lorraine, oversaw the family and ran a tight ship. Since his aunts and uncles were so much older, his place in the family was unique and often lonely. He discovered early on that most sports came easily to him. He played varsity football in high school. After graduation, he briefly attended college before becoming interested in jai alai. It is fast, dangerous, and requires extraordinary skill and stamina. Tom had both in abundance. He learned the sport quickly, turned pro after several years, and enjoyed a successful career, which ended soon after he met Jennifer.

Back upstairs, we sifted through other papers from an album that he produced. Mixed among them was the condolence letter that Bill Negron had written to Tom's grandparents several days after his father's death. Tom had mentioned it during our first phone conversation four years earlier. I picked it up and read it. Two things immediately caught my eye. The first was that it was typed. The second was, seeing the date, that it had been written less than a week after the LZ Loon Battle. I couldn't imagine how Bill had found the time, empathy, or typewriter to have written several dozen thoughtful personal letters while, at the same time, leading us on the summer assaults of hill after hill.

After a thoughtful reconstruction of the circumstances that led to Tom's death, Bill wrote:

I and every other man in Company "C" knew and loved Tom. Because of his record, his diligence, his professionalism, he became a key man in his platoon and each platoon member regarded him as a selfless leader and one whom they would gladly follow. It may somehow soften the helpless grief I know that both of you feel to know that Thomas's many friends have wept for him and are praying for him. We all deeply feel his loss.

The other items he shared with me that afternoon evoked feelings that bored directly into my heart. I recognized, from Norma's descriptions, several of the pictures that she said Lorraine had taken from her when she took her son. I thought it would be important for Norma to see everything that was there, so I asked Tom if I could have them scanned. He agreed without hesitation. I gathered the pictures, letters, and telegrams and drove to a nearby Staples to have the whole lot downloaded onto a thumb drive. When I returned, Charlie's anxious face was pressed against the glass of the storm door, eagerly awaiting my return. It was getting late and nearing time for us to get on the road.

Before leaving, I asked about his grandparents, aunts, and uncles. He said that both his grandfather and grandmother had died five years before. Through the years, he had remained close to his uncle George, his father's older brother, and his lifelong partner. George had recently died. He said that he had gone on occasional family trips with his uncle Al and had pleasant memories of those. The other aunts and uncles and even his grandparents, while still alive, had not been a part of his life for many years.

"It was like I'd been orphaned twice," Tom told me. "That's how it felt. I haven't spoken to any of them since my grand-mother's funeral."

Throughout the day, Norma's name was mentioned only once. After Jennifer told a story about one of several run-ins that she'd had with Lorraine when she and Tom were dating, I recounted a story that Norma had told me about one of her many confrontations. She had told me that Lorraine had once slammed the front door in her face after telling her to stay away from her son. When I said this, Jennifer laughed out loud and looked over at Tom. "Oh yeah," she said, "that happened to me too. When Tom and I were dating, I stopped by the house and rang the doorbell. Lorraine answered, looked me in the eye and said, 'You stay away from my son,' and slammed the door in my face." I asked her what she had done then, and Jennifer replied, "I rang the doorbell again. Lorraine answered it again. I told her to never do that to me again and walked past her and into the house to see Tom."

It had been an intense day. Charlie and I had enjoyed being their guests from the moment we arrived. Whether chatting around the kitchen counter, eating lunch outside on the patio, or lingering in the living room during the afternoon, the five of us had moved seamlessly from spot to spot in a close knot. No one was ever out of earshot.

As we walked to the front door, I told Tom about our annual Charlie Company gathering on Knotts Island. "These guys all knew your dad," I said, "some better than I did. We'd love to have you come. If you can get yourself there, we'll take care of the rest." He nodded and said that he'd think about it. I then said the words that I'd wanted to say all day. "Tom, you should get to know your mother. She's a lovely woman. She and I have become friends. I think that you would like her too. You remind me a lot of each other."

Tom stood back ever so slightly and looked me squarely in the eyes. "Jack, I'm married. I have two teenaged kids. One's going to college next year. I'm working two jobs. I can't fit anything else into my life right now. Maybe someday, but not now. And besides," he said after a long pause, "where has she been all these years?"

The words stung. It was a fair question. I thought about the trumped-up custody hearing. I thought about the cards, letters, and presents that had been sent and returned unopened. I thought about Norma's long walks up the hill to the Morrissey house to visit her infant son, only to be told that he could not be disturbed.

"Tom," I replied, "we weren't there."

After we left, I called Bill Negron in Arizona to tell him about the visit. He was eager to hear every detail. When I mentioned reading the condolence letter that he had written, he asked if I could send him a copy. I told him I would.

"Bill," I then said, "I'm curious. How were you able to write all those intensely personal letters to all of those families so soon after the LZ Loon battle?" Then, almost as an afterthought, I added, "And … typed? I won't even ask how you did that."

I knew well from my own experience that the Marine Corps leaves little to chance when it comes to the behavior of its troops. In boot camp, we not only learned how to close-order drill, fire a rifle, and obey orders, we also learned the Marine Corps way to clip our toenails, brush our teeth, spit-shine our shoes, and wipe our backsides. There was a procedure for everything. We were to assume nothing. As Staff Sergeant Hilton, our senior drill instructor, often reminded us, "Assumption, maggots, is the mother of all fuck-ups."

In response to my question, Bill replied, "It's one of the first things that they teach new officers at the Basic School, Jack. Among the greatest responsibilities bestowed on a Marine Corps officer is that of establishing and maintaining timely correspondence with the families of the fallen."

I've since recounted this story to several active-duty and retired Marine Corps officers. Their responses, almost line for line, were always the same.

Katelin, Jennifer, Thomas IV, & Thomas Morrissey III

CHAPTER 36

July 2014, Sanford

When I arrived at the family cottage that evening, I was warmly greeted by Roz, our three daughters, and five grandchildren (now including Niko and Ferdie.) They were eager to hear the news of my visit with Tom and his family. I showed them the pictures I had taken that afternoon. They had seen my pictures of Norma and heard me retell her story over the years, but the sight of her handsome grown son and his beautiful family was almost more than they could bear.

After five relaxing days, I interrupted Charlie's hunt for sea otters and set out on the now-familiar drive to Norma's house. I was eager to see her. I had twenty photographs of Tom and his family on my computer. I couldn't gauge what Norma's reaction might be, but I knew that we were on the brink of a moment we wouldn't have dared imagine four years earlier.

I pulled into Norma's driveway, saw Debra's car, and knew it would again be the three of us. Charlie leapt out, took care of his business, and darted up the steps to the kitchen door. I walked up behind him as Norma emerged to welcome us. Debra was standing beside her. We smiled and hugged. Any unease that we might have felt during our first visit had long since vanished. We were now three friends who were about to share a lovely summer Sunday together. Except this day would be different.

Once we had settled onto the living room sofa with drinks and snacks, I pulled out my laptop and placed it on the coffee table. As I turned it on, Norma and Debra scooched up on either side of me to get closer to the emerging images. Then there he was—Norma's bright-eyed, forty-seven-year-old son, Tom. Jennifer, Thomas IV, and Katelin were by his side, standing in front of the tall pine trees in their back yard. All four were smiling with a warmth and vitality that leapt off the screen.

Norma hadn't seen her son since he was a baby. Katelin looked older and lovelier than her most recent Facebook picture. It was the first time she had seen a photograph of her grandson, Thomas, and her daughter-in-law, Jennifer. The two sisters wanted to cherish that first picture for as long as they could. They were reluctant to let me click on to the next one as they swapped observations about each detail.

"He looks like his grandfather."

"She's more beautiful than her pictures."

"Look at his hair. Look at *her* hair."

"She looks like her mother."

"Tom looks like his uncle."

"He has his father's eyes."

We began the journey through my pictures slowly, deliberately, and at times agonizingly. The two women sat spellbound as forty-six years evaporated before their teary eyes. We were emotionally drained by the time we took a break for lunch. Norma and Deb had provided a narrative throughout, telling story after story about Tom when he was a baby. They couldn't stop except to laugh, shake their heads, and continue with another story; the day he came home from the hospital, his love of Cheetos, the afternoon he began to crawl, and the time he took his first steps. The flowing stories evoked joy and laughter. The floodgates had opened.

The horrors of those awful days in 1968 were eclipsed by the love she had felt for her beautiful child and the joy he had brought to her and her late husband. Debra was six years younger than Norma and had lived through every moment of little Tom's life with her sister. She had changed his diapers and fed him supper while Norma was at work. She had bounced him on her knee, taken him for walks into town, tucked him in at night, and been lulled to sleep by his soft, rhythmic breathing. When the first picture filled the screen, both women momentarily forgot the years of shared anguish, pain, hatred, and fear.

The rest of the day passed in a flash. I had more questions, which led Norma to unearth more long-dormant memories. Debra quietly listened and added her own anecdotes. There were things that Norma remembered and things she didn't remember. Occasionally, if I pushed, she would shake her head in frustration and again say, "Jack, it was over fifty years ago."

Before I left, Norma and I walked around her backyard. The vegetable garden was in full production. I was impressed. We strolled back to admire the flower garden that was blooming with azaleas, daisies, bee balm, echinacea, and tiger lilies. Charlie was becoming restless, so we walked back to the house, gathered our things, and got ready to leave. Before we did, I turned to Norma. I needed to take a chance with one parting thought.

"Norma," I began, "Tom knows I'm here. I've showed him your picture. He knows that you know I spent time with him and his family earlier this week. He knows I was going to show you the pictures of my visit. So, everybody knows everything." I paused to be certain that she was following me before I continued. "You're the mom, so perhaps you should take the first step. Send him a card—a simple card, nothing too flowery or sappy. I'll give you his address." I held my breath, waiting for her response. I thought I was wading into uncharted territory, but thought it was time.

"Okay … maybe …" she responded tentatively. "Deb and I are going up to Ellsworth tomorrow for a family reunion. I'll get one when we get back next week."

"Oh, come on," I playfully protested. "Go this afternoon. Go into town, get it, write it, and send it on its way. Then you may have a reply by the time you get back."

A small, knowing smile crossed Norma's lips, like a child caught doing something silly. "Okay," she said, "I'll do it this afternoon."

Charlie and I loaded up the car for the trek back to Fort Lee, gave final hugs and waves, backed out of the driveway, and headed for home. Six hours later, I sat down at my desk and opened a waiting email from Norma. It contained a picture of the card that she had sent to her son. She was putting herself out there. The time had come.

I waited a week before sending her an inquiring email. Had she heard anything from Tom?

"No. Nothing," she responded.

Another week—still nothing.

Having recently seen Tom, I thought of calling him with a fatherly admonition, "Write your mother!" But that was quickly followed by a moment of doubt. I had inserted myself deeply into both of their lives. Now, because of my prodding, Norma had opened herself up to more suffering and pain. I was discouraged and mad at myself.

The following week, on July 19, 2013, nearly three years after the VVA had filed my appeal, I received a letter from the Department of Veterans Affairs informing me that the Veterans Board of Appeals had acted favorably on my appeal. My PTSD rating was raised to 70 percent, so with my overall rating now over 100 percent, I was deemed to be unemployable. My monthly disability payment was increased, and I received a lump-sum distribution for the thirty-four months since the original filing date of September 10, 2010.

After calling the bank to be certain that the funds had been deposited, I pulled out my checkbook and paid off all my debts. It was an enormous relief. I thought of Margaret and the VVA lawyers who had skillfully presented my case to the Board of Appeals. I thought of the kind clerk in Newark VA office who had been so helpful during my intermittent visits to her office. I thought of the photograph of the thousands of paper files, mine being but one, that had been so precariously stacked in the Winston-Salem claims office. Finally, I thought of what it meant for me. While I was by no means rich, I was optimistically aware that if I continued to live a frugal life, I would never again owe anybody anything.

But for occasional Facebook posts, I'd had little contact with Norma or Tom since my visits the previous summer. I was giving them both a wide berth. In February 2014, I sent Tom an email to remind him about the Knotts Island Charlie Company reunion that was a month away. I had little confidence that he would be able to find the time to attend, but still held out hope. I received no response for two weeks, which was not uncommon. By his own admission, Tom wasn't good at staying in touch.

One evening, however, he called.

"Jack, it's Tom," he began. "Hey, I just read your email. Sorry. You know I don't check it that often. About the reunion," he continued, "is the invitation still open? I'd like to come if I can swing it."

"That's great, Tom, of course you can still come," I responded. "I'm thrilled."

"What are the dates again?" he asked.

After I replied, I heard him whispering something. This was followed by the sound of clicking computer keys. I could picture Jennifer on her laptop, close by his side, checking flight dates and times. She found connections that would get him there on Friday morning and take him back home the following Monday. I told him that I would pick him up at the Norfolk airport when he arrived and drop him off for the flight home.

After we hung up, I sat back in my chair and stared off into space. *The Morrissey family*, I thought to myself, *is the gift that keeps on giving.* I got back on the phone and shared the news with Terry Tillery and several other buddies who would be at the reunion. The responses were immediate and enthusiastic. "That's great." "No shit." "Really?" "Morrissey's kid?" I was glad I'd thought to mention it to Tom the previous summer. It had been an afterthought. Now I tried to anticipate the scene. We were all a generation older than Tom. Would he fit in? What insights might he gain into his father's Marine Corps experience? The answers to these and other questions hung in the air. Tom was putting himself out there. It was going to be a remarkable weekend.

Two days later, I got an email from Norma. The coincidence was uncanny. We had not corresponded for months.

> Just checking in, haven't heard from you. I hope your holidays were special and you are surviving this brutal winter.
>
> I haven't heard anything from Tom and really not expecting to. I had hoped he would be more open-minded.
>
> I thought perhaps, if you would not mind of course, that I could employ you to deliver a few of his dad's personal items. Purple Heart, medals, watch, lighter, etc. small items. You would make a great person for the job! It's just something I would like taken care of before I leave this earth.
>
> If you would rather not, I certainly understand.
>
> Hope you are well. Best wishes for a happy spring.

I wrote her back, relayed my recent conversation with Tom, and told her that if she could get the box to me by the following week, I would take it with me to North Carolina. She wrote back the following day.

Please tell Tom that his dad's watch was very special to him. I almost hate to send it, as I feel close to him having it here. Also, the lighter, silly as it sounds. When I was down, I would hold that lighter so tight. Just knowing Tom held it made me feel better.

I sensed sadness in her note or perhaps it was wistfulness. She expressed regret that there had been some minor damage to several of the items when they had been sent from Vietnam. She was also sorry that, over the years, there had been some slight mildew damage.

The small, tightly wrapped, package arrived in Fort Lee two days before I departed for Knotts Island.

CHAPTER 37

March 2014, Knotts Island

Tom arrived at Norfolk International Airport on Friday morning. I was glad to see him. He looked well and was eager to meet the others. With several hours to kill while waiting for another member of our group to arrive, we found a diner and had breakfast.

When we returned to the car, I reached into the back seat and pulled out a black leather motorcycle vest that was covered with Vietnam War and Marine Corps patches. Although I'd had it for several years, I thought it might help Tom feel like part of the group when he gathered with the boys.

"Here, Tom," I said, handing it to him, "this is for you."

He examined the vest carefully, regarded each patch, then stepped out of the car and slipped it on. "Thanks, Jack. How do I look?" he asked with a smile while straightening it out.

"Like one of us," I replied, because he did. We were off to a good start.

We went back to the airport and met Don Shelhouse, a former Charlie Company marine who had served with Tom's dad in the second platoon. I had not seen Greg since Vietnam, but we recognized each other at first glance and shared a big hug. I introduced him to Tom. He had not heard that he would be joining us.

"You're Morrissey's kid?" he asked. "No shit. I loved your dad. He was a great guy." He then paused for several seconds and broke into a big smile. "I remember one time when your dad got a picture of you, and your hair was getting kind of long. He said he couldn't wait to get home and get you a haircut. Guess he wouldn't have to worry about that now." He laughed. Tom's hairline had well receded.

When we got to Knotts Island an hour later, we were warmly greeted by the other recent arrivals. All were delighted to see Tom. It was apparent that I needn't have been concerned about his mixing in with a bunch of Vietnam veterans. Most of the group stayed in the old duck-hunting lodge that we'd used in previous years. Tom and I were fortunate to be the houseguests of Nancy and Terry Tillery, who had finally built a house to go with the garage. When we gathered as a group, everyone had a story to tell about Tom's dad and his assistant gunner, George Hughes. Most were funny. I kept Tom in my sight but needn't have. He might well have been his father in the way that he easily slipped into the group and absorbed it all. Occasionally I'd hear part of a conversation.

"Hi. What brings you here this weekend?" The question came from Terry Tillery's sister-in-law, Becky, who had joined us for a Saturday evening gathering at a local bar.

"My dad was in Charlie Company," Tom responded.

"Which one is he?" she asked, while slowly scanning the crowded room.

"He's not here. He was killed on LZ Loon."

A pause. "Oh, I am so sorry. So, you never knew him?"

"No. I was a baby when he was killed."

"Did you come with your mother?"

"No," said Tom, "I came down with Jack. I don't know my mother."

"You don't know your mother?" she queried with empathy.

It was a tender conversation. I didn't hear the rest but could see that Tom's story was becoming known. During the evening, several people came over to me and asked, "So, what's the deal with the kid's mother?"

One stroke of good fortune was the presence of Charlie Company veteran Harold Wilson and his son-in-law, Byron Moore. Harold had arrived in-country as a Loon replacement shortly after I had left. Byron had learned that Harold had been a marine in Vietnam years after he had married Harold's daughter, Kim. He was fascinated and began to spend hours probing Harold for stories. As Harold began to connect with our Charlie Company brothers, he'd invite us to come visit with him and his family at their home in Marion, North Carolina. Byron absorbed every detail and became our unofficial historian. He now knows more about the *who*, *what*, and *where* of Charlie Company during that period than anyone. Hardly a day goes by when we don't get an email from Byron heralding some little-remembered fact or welcoming "another brother found." Byron's wife, Kim, was conceived in Hawaii during Harold's R&R in 1969. At our gatherings, she wears a T-shirt that proudly states, "Made in Hawaii."

Tom and Byron hit it off. They were about the same age, and although neither had served with us, they were as much a part of the company as we were. Byron wanted to know everything there was to know about Tom's father, and Tom was eager to know as much as he could about that period in Charlie Company's history. It could not have gone any better.

We all had breakfast together at the lodge on Sunday morning before the boys began to depart for home. Tom was included in the goodbyes and received a hug from every marine. Robert Rodriguez was among the last to leave. Rod, born and raised in San Marco, Texas, by a tight, loving family, had been a second platoon squad leader and a close friend of Tom's father. Standing five feet nine, Rod carried the same well-toned body and stoic expression that he bore in Vietnam. He looked like he hadn't gained a pound. We all had great respect for Rod. He was an outstanding marine who had mentored many of us under combat conditions. A demanding taskmaster, he expected the best from each marine under his command.

Long after he had gone home, several of us, when faced with a vexing situation under fire or on patrol, would quietly ask ourselves, "What would Rod do?"

After throwing his bag in the back of his truck, Rod turned, slowly approached Tom, and looked directly into his eyes. "I was glad to meet you, Tom," he said as he put forth his right hand.

"Thanks, Rod," Tom replied extending his own right hand to meet Rod's. "I was glad to meet you too. Thank you for all the things you said about my dad. I've learned more about him this weekend than I ever knew."

"Sure," Rod replied. "He was a good man and a good marine. He was also my friend. When we were in the bush, I never worried when your dad was nearby." Rod, a man of few words, paused, pressed a little closer, and continued. "Look, Tom, you've got a mother. She brought you into this world. I don't know what happened back then and don't give a shit. Neither should you. She's your mother. We only get one. Not one of us is going to live forever—not you, not me, and not your mother. Get to know her while there is still time, Tom."

That evening, after everyone had left, Tom and I returned to the Tillery house, where Nancy was preparing a spaghetti dinner. We were exhausted. After breaking open a bottle of wine, the four of us collapsed in the living room. Nancy and Terry then gave me an expectant look. It was time.

"Here, Tom," I said, "I've got something for you."

With that, I picked up Norma's well-taped box and handed it to him. He noted that it was addressed to me in Fort Lee and that it had been sent by his mother in Sanford. He slowly and deliberately slit open the top, pulled out some packing, and carefully removed a padded case. Inside was his father's Purple Heart, along with a signed letter from the president of the United States. He looked over at me as he removed more packing and produced another case of similar size. Inside was his father's Bronze Star medal with the **V** designation for valor in combat and a signed letter from the commandant of the Marine Corps. The next case he removed contained his dad's Vietnam Service Medal.

Tom paused, looked over at me, and said, "Well, I guess those weren't my father's medals that my grandfather gave to me, after all."

I wanted to laugh, but it wasn't funny.

Among the other treasures to emerge was his father's watch, which he held gently, wound carefully, and placed on his wrist. I passed on his mother's message about how much the watch had meant to his father. Next came the Zippo lighter that was engraved, "Tom Morrissey, Norfolk Sentry of the Month, April 1967." I was reminded of the peace that Norma said the lighter had brought her over the years. There were several other items. He passed each one through his fingers before he placed it on the table in front of him. It was as though he felt his father in each one. When he had finished, he gazed at the three of us.

"Thank you," he said. "I don't know what else to say."

"You're welcome," the three of us mumbled as one. We had no more idea of what to say than he did.

I drove Tom to the Norfolk airport the next morning on my way home. We were quiet during the hourlong trip. It had been an emotional and exhausting weekend. We got out of the car at curbside and pulled his bag out of the back. Tom smiled and looked right at me.

"Look, Jack," he said, holding up his wrist. "It still works!" Indeed, his father's watch was ticking away. I smiled. We hugged. We thanked each other. We hugged again. As we parted, he looked back and said, "I want you to know that I'm going to get in touch with my mother."

I smiled. "Good, Tom. That's good news." Then, as he turned to leave, I said, "Tom." I then paused and asked, "Tom, what did it?" I waited for another moment before continuing, "What made you decide to get in touch with her now?"

"Rodriguez," he responded without so much as a blink.

When I got home that afternoon, I emailed Norma the pictures that I had taken of Tom with her late husband's Vietnam buddies. I included several of him opening the box. I didn't tell her that Tom was going to get in touch with her. I was excited by the prospect, but cautious. I didn't want to set her up for another fall.

The following Thursday, after three days of wrenching curiosity, I received an email from Norma.

> A quick message to let you know Tom reached out to me on Facebook chat. He thanked me for the box and said it meant the world to him. I kept the conversation going and we covered some ground. He feels overwhelmed and said he has shed a lot of tears this past week … unanswered questions, etc. He feels as though he has missed out on a lot. We will plan to meet when the weather gets warmer.
>
> Jack, I hope you realize that you are the angel that made all of this happen. Tom says his dad sent you to him.

Norma and Tom exchanged several Facebook posts during the next week. She became friends with Katelin and Thomas, which allowed a vivid journal of their everyday lives to open before her. It was intoxicating. She found herself sitting by the computer for most of those days, waiting for the next *ding*.

The following Sunday, Norma and Tom spoke for the first time in forty-six years. They were both nervous and tentative but kept the conversation going as the other three Massachusetts Morrisseys huddled around trying to hear every word. The phone was passed from family member to family member so that each could speak with Tom's long-estranged mother. As the conversation concluded they agreed to meet when the weather got warmer.

Norma sent me a note after the conversation. She told me about their plans to get together and asked if I would attend. She felt that my presence might make Tom feel more comfortable. A week later, Norma wrote that she and Tom had spoken several more times and that he was sounding more relaxed. "He even jokes a little," she said. They decided that Norma would host the reunion at her house. Tom wanted Jen and his children to be there. Norma wanted her sisters, Debra and Karen, to attend.

Norma and I agreed that Tom had long been aware of his grandmother's shortcomings and his grandfather's drinking problem. More recently, he had told me that he had felt abandoned by his adopted family. "Twice an orphan," was how he put it. Emotions on both sides were hovering near the surface and would have to be treated with care. Norma still felt deep hatred for Lorraine, who had been so viciously cruel to her before and after Tom was born.

I had found several pieces of correspondence in Tom's scrapbook that added additional tidbits of information to the terrible events in the spring of 1968, including several legal documents related to the custody hearing. When I showed the scanned copies of them to Norma, she was furious. The long-held bile rose to the surface as she released a vituperative tirade at this woman who had now been dead for nearly ten years. When she calmed down, she expressed concern that the depth of her feelings might betray her intent to be positive in her reconciliation with Tom. That was the last thing she wanted. Norma understood that for her family to be brought back together, she and her son would have to look forward rather than back. Neither Tom nor Norma had caused the situation, and neither could change what had happened. Norma apologized to me for her vehement venting about Lorraine. I laughed softly and told her that I'd always be willing to be the recipient of such outbursts so long as they were directed at me and not at Tom.

I hoped that, over time, the pain of the loss and separation that Norma and Tom had endured would be replaced by a shared future that would be filled with joy and fresh possibilities.

I didn't dare to think otherwise.

Knotts Island. Back row: Robert Rodriguez, Bill Matthews, Thomas J. Morrissey III, Harold Wilson, & Bill Murphy, Front row: Ron Layman, Terry Tillery, Don Shelhouse, & Jack McLean

CHAPTER 38

May 2014, Sanford

On the morning of May 17, 2014, Charlie and I drove north from Massachusetts into New Hampshire on the final leg of our trip to Sanford. The reunion was set to take place at 11 a.m. I felt calm and at peace. I didn't want the drive to end. I wanted to immerse myself in the memories—good and bad—that had brought me to this place.

Passing the exit for Hampton Beach, I recalled Tom's stories of his joyful summer days there half a century before. The long-shuttered Pease Air Force Base was soon off to our left. Pease had been the planned destination for Norma and her friend Peggy on the snowy February afternoon in 1964 when, while sitting in the back seat of Barry Bittner's car, she first saw Tom. Prior to crossing the Piscataqua River into Maine, we passed the exit for the town of Portsmouth, the site of Tom's enlistment into the Marine Corps and, three years later, the place where Norma, overcome with grief, had received his remains.

My plan had been to reach Norma's house by ten thirty, so we'd have time to talk prior to Tom's arrival. We drove down the hill into Sanford, past the abandoned mills, across the Mousam River, and back up the other side. It was a bustling Saturday morning. I saw pickup trucks parked in front of the hardware store. Families, with children in tow, were pulling into the McDonald's parking lot, and carloads of uniformed kids were being driven to and from soccer practice. I'd somehow expected that the world should have stopped in its place on this day, much as it had for me, but of course, it hadn't. Life was going on in this small town, oblivious to the momentous event that was unfolding for one small family a mile up the road.

There were three cars in Norma's driveway when we arrived—one for each of the Morrill sisters. I pulled my car over to one side to leave room for Tom to park. Norma greeted us on the deck by the side door. She was radiant, dressed in dark-khaki cargo pants and a soft cream-colored short-sleeved sweater. It was a lovely warm (for Maine) spring morning. I gazed across the backyard to take in the early blooms in her flower garden. I then turned to see Norma sitting back down at the patio table flanked by her two sisters. As I pulled up a chair to join them, I thought about all she had been through with their loving support. I thought of the two younger girls and wondered what lasting impression the sad saga had had left on their lives.

I was brought back to the present when I saw Tom's car turn into the driveway. We all rose. Norma then slowly walked off the deck and down to the driveway. The car came to a stop. The four doors opened as one as Tom, Jennifer, Katelin, and Thomas emerged. Tom's was the closest. He stood, looked intently at his approaching mother, and began to walk in her direction. He was wearing light-colored chinos with a soft, green button-down shirt and sunglasses. Neither Norma nor Tom broke stride until they came together and fell into a full embrace. Tom wrapped his arms tightly around his mother's waist as Norma reached up and clutched her son by the shoulders and neck. They remained that way, frozen, for several minutes. Finally, Norma drew her head back, looked him in the eyes, and whispered something. They smiled and resumed their embrace for several more minutes.

After introductions were made and greetings exchanged, we moved up the steps, through the kitchen, and into the living room. Drinks and snacks appeared. All at once everyone was talking at the same time. For the first hour, Norma and Tom sat on the sofa, hunched together over the coffee table, looking through their opened scrapbooks, which had pictures and memorabilia from the two families. They were oblivious to the rest of us. Tom would point to something and ask a question. Norma would respond as she pointed to something else.

While their expressions were serious and focused, I did see occasional smiles. Later I noticed that they were holding hands. Now and then, I'd hear one of their voices rise above the rest, but for the most part, they were speaking to each other in tones no louder than whispers. Among the items that

Norma shared with her son were legal letters and records of the court proceedings from the custody fight in 1968. She also produced several of the returned birthday cards and letters that she had sent him over the years.

After a time, Norma stood, walked over to Katelin, and gave her a small box. "Here," she said, "I'd like you to have this." We all silently watched as Katelin carefully unwrapped the package, opened the box, and removed a gold ring. She was stunned and looked to her grandmother for guidance.

"It's my wedding ring," Norma said. "You should have it."

Eyes were moistening.

After a pause, Debra went to Katelin and handed her a wrapped rectangular box. "Here," she said. "This is something else for you." Katelin looked up and thanked her. What emerged from the wrapping was a traditionally dressed Vietnamese doll inside of a glass case. "It's from your grandfather," she continued. "He sent it to me from Vietnam when I was fourteen. I want you to have it."

After several more minutes, Debra approached Thomas with a small, wrapped envelope. "Here, Thomas," she said. "I'd like you to have this." Thomas unwrapped several layers of paper and found a 1964 dime tucked inside. "I was hysterical when your grandfather was leaving for Vietnam," she explained. "No one could stop me from crying. He reached into his pocket and gave me that," she said, pointing to the dime in Thomas's hand. "He told me that nothing bad would happen to him as long as I held on to it tightly while he was gone." Finally, she produced a bag of Cheetos and, remembering his fondness for the snack when she'd last seen him decades before, handed it to Tom. It was that kind of day.

An abundant buffet lunch was set out in the kitchen. We picked up plates and served ourselves from overflowing platters of food and moved back into the living room to eat. All chatted over each other, so it was a challenge for me to catch the thread of even one of the conversations.

Later in the afternoon, Norma took Tom by the hand and led him out onto the deck and down across the back yard to see her garden. The rest of us followed. Tom then excused himself, walked back to his car, and returned carrying a large potted red rose bush. "Here, Mom," he said, placing it at his mother's feet, "this is for you and your garden."

Norma said, "It's lovely, Tom. Thank you."

Jennifer walked over and said, "I saw a huge pot of beautiful annuals at the garden store, which I thought would be perfect. Tom had agreed, but after admiring them, he said no and walked over to the rose bush."

"Yeah," continued Tom, "I didn't want to get my mother something that was going to die at the end of the summer."

Tom and Norma agreed on a spot for the rose bush at the front and center of her flower bed. Norma walked to the small garden shed and returned with a spade and a bag of fertilizer. Tom dug the hole, carefully knocked the bush out of its pot, and gently placed it into the space he'd created. As he refilled the hole around the plant, Norma sprinkled in the fertilizer. When it was comfortably seated in the ground, Norma brought over the hose, turned it on low, and began to give a good soaking to the special new denizen of her garden. When the planting was done, mother and son proudly posed for photos in front of the blooming bush. It looked right at home. So did the two of them.

A chill crept into the afternoon air, so we made our way back to the deck and into the kitchen. I summoned Charlie and put on his leash. We had a long drive ahead of us. The day's events had taken on a life of their own. I didn't think we'd be missed. As I walked into the living room to gather my things, I noticed, for the first time that day, the picture frame on the shelf, which on past visits had held Katelin's Facebook pictures. The frame now contained a photograph that I had taken of Katelin and Thomas in their back yard the summer before. I thought back to the day that I had first seen Katelin's grainy Facebook picture in that same frame four years earlier. Now the sight of Norma's two handsome grandchildren smiling back at me was more than I could bear. I began to cry.

It had been a remarkable day, well beyond what the three of us might have imagined. Norma had dared to hope but had lost much of her optimism earlier in the spring when she sent me the package of her late husband's Vietnam artifacts to deliver to her son. Tom, long an orphan, feared the hurt of being rejected by the mother he had never known. And I had not let my mind imagine such a day. Early on, it was none of my business. Then it became all my business. Fate had put me in the position to bring this family together. Now waves of joy and satisfaction rippled through my every pore. After decades of pain and lingering horror, it occurred to me that my recovery must now be complete. How else could I have so delicately engineered all that led to this reunion?

Months later, while looking through the photos that I had taken that day, one stood out. After the long embrace in the driveway when they first met, Norma had drawn her head back, looked into Tom's eyes, and whispered something. Curious about what she might have said, I called her.

"Norma?" I asked, "remember that picture I took of you and Tom hugging in the driveway that day—the one where it looks like you are saying something to him?"

"Yes."

"May I ask what you said?"

She gave half a laugh and replied, "Yes. I told him that he looked the same, only bigger." The last time Norma had seen her son, he was fourteen months old.

Summer turned to fall, and a steady flow of good news came down to me from New England. A *real* family reunion had taken place at Karen's house on Lake Winnipesaukee in August. Tom and his family had attended, as did Norma's other two sons. A regular flow of texts, emails, Facebook posts, Instagram photos, and telephone calls were exchanged. Norma visited her son's home in Massachusetts. Katelin began her sophomore year of college on the varsity field hockey team. Thomas entered his junior year of high school. Tom power-washed and painted his mother's house.

Several years later, I ran into Jim Munroe, a dear friend, Andover classmate, and former marine, who had entered the priesthood after his college graduation. Jim, who had baptized each of my three daughters, knew I had long struggled with my faith. In response to his inquiry about what I'd been up to lately, I suggested we sit down. I then told him the whole Morrissey story from start to finish. After a long silence, he stood up, summoned me to do the same, and held me in a long embrace.

"You're in, Jack," he said, standing back from me.

"In?" I responded, unsure of what he meant.

"Yes," he replied, rolling his eyes skyward. "In."

Norma Morrissey & Thomas Morrissey III

CHAPTER 39

January 2015, Dover

On a cold, gray mid-January morning in 2015, I again drove north from Massachusetts into New Hampshire. My destination for this trip was Dover. I had arranged to meet Norma and Tom in the rear parking lot of the Dover Public Library at eleven o'clock. With the reunion eight months behind us, I'd asked Norma if she'd give us a private tour of the town where she and her late husband had met and fallen in love.

Shortly before reaching Dover, I passed the place where, forty-seven years earlier, I had turned around and headed back to Boston. The long-tempered feelings from that day bubbled back up within me. Weeks back from Vietnam, I recalled how inadequate I had felt at the prospect of facing Norma. I also remembered both my guilt for being alive and the shame for having remained in my fighting hole.

That day now seemed far away, particularly since Norma and I had become such good friends. Might circumstances have been different if I *had* completed the journey that day? Perhaps she could have helped shepherd me back to sanity. Perhaps I could have helped her get their son back. We would never know. I had turned around and Tom was still dead.

When I arrived, I observed a scene as tender as one that I might have imagined then—except that Tom was no longer a baby. Mother and child were arm in arm, smiling, and absorbed in their own little world. I could see their breath as they shifted their feet back and forth to keep warm. It occurred to me that this was the first time Norma and Tom had been in Dover together since he was a baby.

I knew the trauma Norma had endured, particularly in the years after Tom was killed. In rapid succession, she had lost her husband and her infant son. "I lived on Valium for three years after that," she once told me. Tom had been an infant at the time and, although he'd lost his mother and father within days of each other, he remembered only that he'd been raised by his grandparents in a house full of older aunts and uncles. Norma had never been discussed in his presence—not even once. He knew that his father had been a war hero and had clung tightly to the few pieces of his memorabilia he'd been given.

After a warm greeting and a brief discussion about the day's itinerary, we begin our pilgrimage at the nearby Dover City Hall. The imposing red-brick Colonial Revival edifice had grand steps, four imposing two-story columns, and a steepled clock tower. Staring up at it, I felt the gravitas of an earlier time when Dover was among the foremost manufacturing locations in the young United States. It was here where Norma and Tom had received their marriage license. It was also here that, days later, they celebrated their wedding at the weekly town dance in the large meeting room.

We climbed the steps, pulled open the heavy door, and entered a large, dimly lit hallway. The sound of our footsteps echoed as we made our way down the silent corridor past the line of frosted glass doors that concealed the town offices. Looming directly ahead, at the end of the long hall, were two dark wooden doors. The sign above them read *Meeting Room*. Beside the door, on the left, was an engraved bronze plaque titled, *Vietnam Honor Roll*. The three of us stood before it in reverent silence. Six lines down, his name stood out.

Morrissey, Thomas J. Jr.

Tom's face appeared serenely in my mind. I knew that he was with us. I knew that he'd also been with us at the reunion in Sanford eight months earlier. *How proud he must be*, I thought, *of the family that he and Norma had created.*

The day had taken on a somber tone, and it had only just begun. Since it was cold and we had a lot of ground to cover, we decided to do the rest of the tour by car. We walked back to the library parking lot and, with me as the driver and Norma as our guide, set out on her journey down Memory Lane. We began on Main Street, where Norma pointed out the spot where she had first spied Tom.

"It was history after that," she had once told me.

Turning left on Church Street, we drove to what had been the Morrills' home on Park Street. I tried to imagine Norma along with her son, mother, and two sisters squeezed into that multifamily home. Further down the street, we passed the former Dover Footwear factory where Norma had worked and where Tom came to visit every day at lunchtime. She then led us down the river to what had been the Sawyer Mills parking lot, where she and Tom had shared their first kiss. Crossing the Cochecho River below the falls, we drove up the long hill and parked in front of the old Morrissey house on Lexington Street. I thought about Tom in his tuxedo, backing out of that driveway on prom night, as he set off to meet Norma in Bangor. I shivered at the recollection of Norma walking up that same hill, time after time, to see her son, only to have Lorraine slam the door in her face.

After lunch, we drove to our final stop—St. Mary's Cemetery on Dover Point Road. After getting out of the car, Norma took her son's hand, and they walked in the direction of her husband's grave. Both were familiar with the route, since they had each visited the plot over the years. In all that time, however, neither had been aware of the other's presence.

Norma and her son knelt silently by Tom's grave for several moments. I stood behind them. It was the first time I'd been in Tom's presence since the afternoon of June 5, 1968.

Another brother found.

Gazing at the two of them kneeling there, I felt fortunate to have played a role in bringing this family back together. Mostly, however, I felt a powerful sense of honor that I had fulfilled the sacred promise to my fallen Marine Corps brother.

Semper fidelis, Tom.

We did not leave you behind.

Thomas J. Morrissey Jr grave

ACKNOWLEDGMENTS

My decades-long recovery came at the expense of many people—family and friends—who remain dear to me. I wrote this book as a testament to them and their understanding that writing was integral to my post-traumatic recovery. I believe my story will benefit other victims of both post-traumatic stress and Agent Orange exposure.

Roz McLean never wavered in her encouragement and support. She and our three daughters, Sarah McLean, Martha Magrina, and Sylvia Elmer, not only lived much of this story, but were also eager and active participants in all elements of this book's creation. Thank you each with love from the bottom of my heart.

Karen McLean bore much of the brunt of my recovery. At her suggestion, I wrote my first book, *Loon: A Marine Story*. That journey took its toll on both of us. It also led me into the capable psychological care of the Department of Veterans Affairs Medical Center in Washington, DC. Thank you, Karen.

Don McLean, Ruth Lizotte, and Barbara O'Neil, my three siblings, have long been unconditional supporters of me and my writing. My love and thanks to each of you.

Critical to the telling of this story were Norma Morrissey and Thomas J. Morrissey III. From our earliest meetings, they shared their difficult family history without condition or reservation. That they didn't change a word of the manuscript, much of it dealing with the heart-wrenching details of their early lives, remains extraordinary to me. They too wanted the story told. Loving thanks to you both and to your wonderful family—Jennifer, Katelin, and Thomas IV.

Key to the early structure of the book was my friend Carl P. Herrmann, who read, reread, then read again every word for detail and accuracy with a thoroughness that (he knew) the author rarely possessed. Thanks, Carl.

Marine Corps buddy Terry Tillery, his wife Nancy, and his mother, Helen Joseph, added immeasurably through Terry and Nancy's recollections of our shared recovery and Helen's incredible letter to me that is included here. Thank you, Tillery's. Another buddy, Buck Willingham shared the heartfelt note written by his wife, Janie, that is also shared here. Thank you, Janie and Buck.

Gil Sanborn and Susan Hackley have thoughtfully coaxed, cajoled, and encouraged me at our weekly Zoom meetings for the past three years. Thanks to you both and now to fellow marine Roger Harris for believing in this story and for keeping me focused.

Significant contributions to this book were made by three recently departed giants: Former US senator Max Cleland, writer and author Joseph Galloway, and my dear friend and Skipper Lieutenant Colonel William Negron (USMC Ret.). You were all there when I needed you. Thank you.

When I met my wife Nina seven years ago, I shared with her what I thought was a completed manuscript of this book. She wasn't so sure. Thank you, Nina for your thoughtful guidance, timely criticism, and abiding patience with this writer. I love you. We made it.

Final thanks to Reedsy, whose professional support led me to my superb editor, Joe Pierson, gifted designer, Asya Blue, and marketing maven David Carriere.

ABOUT THE AUTHOR

Jack McLean is the author of *Loon: A Marine Story* (Random House, 2009), a national best-selling memoir about his service in the United States Marine Corps from 1966 to 1968. He served as an infantry corporal in Vietnam in 1967–68. In the fall of 1968, he became the first Vietnam veteran to enter Harvard University.

His thirty-year marketing career began with the New York Mets as the assistant ticket manager. He subsequently held senior positions with the national insurance broker Johnson

& Higgins in Boston, Portland, and Charlotte. He went on to become the founding managing partner of the Greater Washington (DC) Initiative.

Raised in Summit, New Jersey, he is married (Nina), has three daughters (Sarah, Martha, and Sylvia), eleven grandchildren, and one dog (Charlie). He currently resides in Huntington, New York.

Printed in the USA
CPSIA information can be obtained
at www.ICGtesting.com
LVHW051049171123
764119LV00001B/157